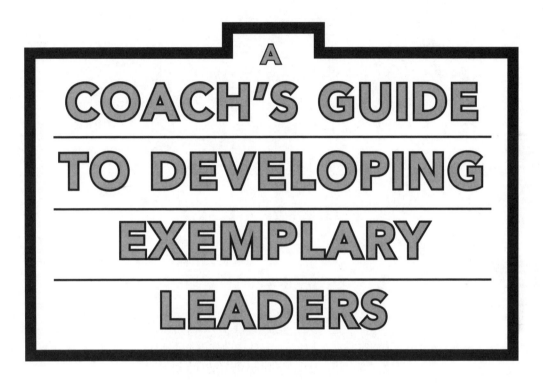

A COACH'S GUIDE TO DEVELOPING EXEMPLARY LEADERS

Second Edition

ABOUT THIS BOOK

WHY IS THIS TOPIC IMPORTANT?

The Leadership Challenge focuses on how to be a successful leader. The Five Practices of Exemplary Leadership® presents five practices that individuals can put into action to bring out the best in themselves and those they lead. Jim and Barry have also identified thirty leadership behaviors that correspond to The Five Practices. Research proves that this content, when put into practice, builds more effective leadership skills, resulting in exemplary leaders. In addition, many Fortune 500 companies see a direct correlation between coaching and excellent leadership skills. This book is important because it ties together these two powerful competencies: the thirty LPI®: Leadership Practices Inventory behaviors and coaching.

WHAT CAN YOU ACHIEVE WITH THIS BOOK?

This book offers you an opportunity to combine two exciting and practical concepts: leadership and coaching. It lays out the basics of Jim and Barry's Five Practices and a failsafe coaching model. When the two are combined, it results in a powerful method to assist leaders to practice leadership skills for reaching excellence.

    The purpose of this book is to provide trainers, consultants, and others working with The Five Practices of Exemplary Leadership® a reliable process to coach leaders.

HOW IS THIS BOOK ORGANIZED?

The book includes eleven chapters divided into two distinct parts. Part I, Coaching to Improve The Five Practices, is written for experienced coaches who have their own coaching process and are looking for ideas (questions, activities, books, or other resources) they can use with clients who have completed the LPI. Chapters 2 through 6 present The Five Practices and introduce dozens of ideas to help a leader improve and increase the frequency of the behaviors that support each.

Part II, Improve Your Coaching Competence, provides an overview of coaching. It is written for someone who is familiar with *The Leadership Challenge*, but wants to learn more about coaching. Chapter 7 presents an overview of coaching, and Chapter 8 allows coaches, new as well as experienced, to assess and improve their coaching skills. Chapter 9 lays out a coaching process that takes a leader from feedback to success. Chapter 10 addresses what to do when things go wrong, and Chapter 11 helps coaches coach themselves to greater heights, providing ideas to improve their skills as well as knowledge about *The Leadership Challenge* concepts.

KOUZES
POSNER

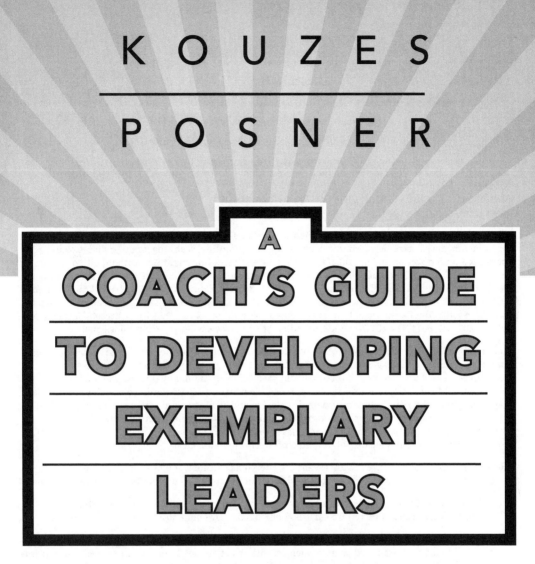

A
COACH'S GUIDE
TO DEVELOPING
EXEMPLARY
LEADERS

Making the Most of
The Leadership Challenge and the
LPI: Leadership Practices Inventory

Second Edition

JAMES M. KOUZES AND BARRY Z. POSNER

WITH ELAINE BIECH

THE
**LEADERSHIP
CHALLENGE**®
A Wiley Brand

For additional copies or bulk purchases of this book or to learn more about The Leadership Challenge®, please contact us toll free at 1-866-888-5159 or by email at leadership@wiley.com.

Wiley also publishes its books in a variety of electronic formats and by print-on-demand. Some material included with standard print versions of this book may not be included in e-books or in print-on-demand. If the version of this book that you purchased references media such as a CD or DVD that was not included in your purchase, you may download this material at http://booksupport.wiley.com.

For more information about Wiley products, visit www.wiley.com.

Library of Congress Cataloging-in-Publication Data has been applied for and is on file with the Library of Congress.
978-1-119-39753-3 (paperback) 978-1-119-42707-0 (ePDF) 978-1-119-42722-3 (ePUB)

Brand Director: William Hull   Manufacturing Supervisor: Becky Morgan
Brand Manager: Marisa Kelley   Development Editor: Susan Monet
Production Editor: Dawn Kilgore   Editor: Rebecca Taff

Printed in the United States of America
SECOND EDITION
Printing 10 9 8 7 6 5 4 3 2 1

CONTENTS

PART I
COACHING TO
IMPROVE THE
FIVE PRACTICES

CHAPTER 1: ACCEPT THE LEADERSHIP CHALLENGE

In This Chapter

- Overview The Leadership Challenge® Model.
- Review The Five Practices of Exemplary Leadership®.
- Review The Ten Commitments of Leadership.
- Introduce how the *LPI®: Leadership Practices Inventory®* supports The Leadership Challenge concept.
- Show the relationship between leadership and coaching.
- Present a way to use this book to coach others based on their LPI results.

Leadership and coaching go hand-in-hand. Both are relationship-based. The Five Practices of Exemplary Leadership can easily describe the practices of an Exemplary Coach.

- A leader must Model the Way; a coach must be an excellent role model for leaders or other clients.
- A leader must Inspire a Shared Vision; a coach must co-create a common vision with the leader.
- A leader must Challenge the Process; a coach must challenge the leader to test his/her own skills and to hold the leader accountable to set and achieve goals.
- A leader must Enable Others to Act; a coach must enable the leader to empower and develop others in the workplace, understand setbacks, and encourage choices.
- A leader must Encourage the Heart; a coach must express confidence in a leader's ability and celebrate successful accomplishments.

As you can see, there are many similarities. When we first envisioned this book, we imagined that there are

- Many individuals who want to be exemplary leaders but may not know how to develop themselves.
- People who have lots of knowledge about how to implement The Five Practices to be good leaders, but may not be sure about how to coach leaders who have busy schedules and may not have time to attend classes.
- Coaches who have lots of knowledge about how to coach others to improve their leadership skills, but who may not know about *The Leadership Challenge*, The Five Practices, or the *LPI: Leadership Practices Inventory*.

A Coach's Guide to Developing Exemplary Leaders was born of these premises. The book addresses these needs.

WHAT DO LEADERS DO WHEN THEY ARE AT THEIR BEST?

The Leadership Challenge and all of its subsequent products are based on continuing research that started more than thirty years ago. We asked thousands of people to complete a Personal-Best Leadership Questionnaire, which was developed to learn what people do daily to rally their people and inspire them to work toward a common future.

We conducted our research with an assumption that turns out to be important: We did not have to survey only the best leaders in the best organizations to identify best practices. We assumed that we would find success patterns by asking ordinary people to describe extraordinary experiences. We were right.

After initial research, we developed a personal-best leadership survey of thirty-eight open-ended questions such as:

- Who initiated the project?
- How were you prepared for this experience?
- What special techniques and strategies did you use to involve other people in the project?
- What did you learn about leadership from this experience?

Over a four-year period, we conducted almost six hundred of these surveys and started to implement a shorter survey. Since then we have expanded the research and collected thousands of additional cases, including community leaders, student leaders, church leaders, government leaders, and hundreds of others in non-managerial positions.

Every person we spoke with had at least one leadership story to tell—stories that were rarely textbook cases, but instead were about ordinary people who engage in what has come to be known as The Five Practices of Exemplary Leadership®.

WHAT IS THE LEADERSHIP CHALLENGE MODEL?

The analysis of the personal-best surveys revealed an interesting phenomenon. Even though the individuals' recollections of their peak leadership experiences were all different, all of them engaged in similar practices. We developed a model of leadership that consists of The Five Practices of Exemplary Leadership® we identified earlier:

- Model the Way
- Inspire a Shared Vision
- Challenge the Process
- Enable Others to Act
- Encourage the Heart

The research led us to write our first book, *The Leadership Challenge,* now in its sixth edition, and to develop a quantitative 360-degree instrument, the *LPI: Leadership Practices Inventory*, to measure the five leadership practices. *The Leadership Challenge* has sold over two million copies and has been translated into numerous languages. The LPI is one of the most widely used leadership assessment instruments in the world. More than seven hundred doctoral dissertations and master's theses have been based on The Five Practices of Exemplary Leadership® model.

THE FIVE LEADERSHIP PRACTICES

Let's review The Five Practices.

Model the Way

Leaders know that to gain commitment and to win respect they need to become exemplars of the behavior they expect of others. Excellent leaders need to identify and articulate their personal values—what they represent. People follow people, not words on paper, so leaders must demonstrate that they stand behind their values and demonstrate that they mean what they say with action. The principles that leaders establish, espouse, and live become the standards of excellence for others to follow. The leader who sets an example creates a situation making it easier to build consensus on shared values no matter what the climate. The excellent leader is clear about his or her values and principles because he or she asks for feedback about his or her actions.

Inspire a Shared Vision

A vision is not about a statement; it is about the shared dream of the future. Leaders envision the preferred future, creating an ideal image of the organization or project. They get others behind the vision by vividly expressing their passion. Leaders are able to bring their vision to everyone's level, breathing life into other individuals' hopes and dreams. This strengthens the individuals, strengthens the team, and strengthens the vision. When leaders believe that they can make a difference, others see that the vision can be for the common good of all involved. Excellent leaders incorporate the higher meaning of their work into the vision. This alignment helps others align with the team, the work, and the organization.

Challenge the Process

Leaders look for ways to improve processes, for better, faster, less-expensive ways to get the work done, and they encourage the strength of the team to do it. Leaders make certain that the improvement process has a strong chance of success by helping to develop a logical plan of actions and milestones that incorporates dates, goals, and accountability. Leaders challenge themselves to ensure that they grow and learn. They invariably must experiment and take risks on their way to innovative improvement ideas. This means, of course, that leaders learn from their mistakes and blunders as well as from their successes and triumphs, making it possible for the rest of their team to do the same.

Enable Others to Act

Leaders foster collaboration through the use of excellent interpersonal skills. Developing cooperative relationships, treating others with dignity and respect, and trusting people to do what they say they will builds individuals' self-confidence and capacity to accomplish the team's work. Leaders show respect for others when they consider diverse viewpoints. Leaders involve others in making decisions about how to do their work and they support the ultimate actions. These actions build cooperation across the team. When leaders empower individuals in this way, they ensure that people grow in their jobs, ultimately empowering the entire team.

 ## Encourage the Heart

Leaders bring hope and satisfaction; they bring encouragement and support; and most of all they bring praise and appreciation. People will accomplish extraordinary things when they know someone cares and appreciates their dedication. Leaders recognize the contributions that individuals make; they celebrate the accomplishments that teams make. Leaders begin by showing confidence in individuals' actions. They then continue by praising individuals for both a completed job as well as for achieving small increments along the way. They celebrate creatively, celebrate sincerely, and celebrate often.

THE TEN COMMITMENTS OF LEADERSHIP

Driving The Five Practices are The Ten Commitments of Leadership. It isn't enough—not by a long shot—to list five principles that a leader will follow. The leader must also identify behaviors that support and demonstrate the principles on a daily basis.

Let's briefly review each of these commitments and how leaders are able to demonstrate each.

THE TEN COMMITMENTS

Model the Way

1. Clarify values by finding your voice and affirming shared values.
2. Set the example by aligning actions with shared values.

Inspire a Shared Vision

3. Envision the future by imagining exciting and ennobling possibilities.
4. Enlist others in a common vision by appealing to shared aspirations.

Challenge the Process

5. Search for opportunities by seizing the initiative and by looking outward for innovative ways to improve.
6. Experiment and take risks by consistently generating small wins and learning from experience.

Enable Others to Act

7. Foster collaboration by building trust and facilitating relationships.
8. Strengthen others by increasing self-determination and developing competence.

Encourage the Heart

9. Recognize contributions by showing appreciation for individual excellence.
10. Celebrate the values and victories by creating a spirit of community.

1. Clarify values by finding your voice and affirming shared values.

Leaders must ask themselves, "What do I stand for? What are the principles that guide me in my day-to-day work and keep me here in this job, doing this work, and supporting these people?" Once affirmed, leaders must act out their values, demonstrating what they mean. One of their favorite actions is to engage people in a dialogue about shared values.

2. Set the example by aligning actions with shared values.

Leaders continue to demonstrate their ideas by aligning their actions in everything they do or say. Then they take actions to ensure that their team members understand what is expected of them and how to implement this commitment. When this is achieved, the team's unity leads to shared values. A leader can encourage this by reinforcing behaviors that are consistent with his or her espoused values.

3. Envision the future by imagining exciting and ennobling possibilities.

Developing the capacity to envision the preferred future is a skill that must be both modeled and taught to team members. The leader can reflect on the past, attend to the present, and consider the future, but the leader must also identify the burning passion that will carry the team into the future. Leaders must ask their team members what is motivating them to work toward the vision and to identify their aspirations.

4. Enlist others in a common vision by appealing to shared aspirations.

Leaders listen deeply for how to help team members find a spot for themselves in the future vision. They show team members how they have a role in achieving the exciting shared vision. Leaders create a vision that people can see when they use passionate, visual words that create a clear picture. Leaders must describe their vision and inquire about team members' clarity and desire to take part.

5. Search for opportunities by seizing the initiative and by looking outward for innovative ways to improve.

Leaders keep their eyes and ears open to predict what's on the horizon. This entails looking outside the department and outside the organization. It requires that leaders establish relationships and connect with many sources of information. It also means that leaders must bring their people along by helping them to identify the opportunities that may strengthen the team and the organization. Leaders challenge their team members to find new approaches to old problems.

6. Experiment and take risks by consistently generating small wins and learning from experience.

Experimenting and taking risks is the only path to making innovative improvement. This means that there may be false starts or errors along the way. Even so, leaders cannot give up the opportunities that come with innovation. Leaders can do two things to temper this dilemma. First, they can look to small wins as stepping stones to the ultimate goals. Second, they can celebrate the errors by identifying what the team learned.

7. Foster collaboration by building trust and facilitating relationships.

Leaders create a climate of trust and build relationships by making the first move. Leaders must trust their team if they want the team to trust; they must take steps to build personal interactions if they want the team to do the same. This means that the leader must get out and walk around, talking to team members, finding out about them, and genuinely being interested in them as people, not just as employees. Leaders need to find creative ways to get people to interact on both a personal and professional basis.

8. Strengthen others by increasing self-determination and developing competence.

Leaders develop self-confidence and competence. The two traits are self-perpetuating. The more competent team members are, the higher their self-confidence will be. The higher the team members' self-confidence, the greater the likelihood that they will take a chance at increasing their skill sets. This is a win for everyone involved: individuals become better at what they do, the team becomes stronger, and the leader can increasingly rely on the team to achieve success.

9. Recognize contributions by showing appreciation for individual excellence.

Leaders have a winner's attitude, that is, they believe that people are interested in doing their best in all they do. Thanking people for a job well done, sending a note of appreciation, recognizing someone for living the values—are all easy to do. However, building employees' belief that they can achieve more tomorrow than they are achieving today is the big win for leaders and team members. Leaders find opportunities to show sincere appreciation for team members' accomplishments.

10. Celebrate the values and victories by creating a spirit of community.

Leaders bring people together to celebrate big and little wins. Celebrations perpetuate a corporate spirit of belonging to something greater than one's own being. Leaders find opportunities for celebratory events. Celebrations that link rewards with performance are a powerful way to reinforce achieving the vision. Leaders are successful at this commitment when they find ways to have fun together as a team and make celebrations a part of the team's atmosphere.

These Ten Commitments are more than an action list for aspiring leaders. They are a reminder of the commitment and the responsibility everyone has in the challenging position we call leadership. Leaders need to be aware of how well they are doing with their own leadership commitment. The *Leadership Practices Inventory* can provide that feedback.

HOW DOES THE *LEADERSHIP PRACTICES INVENTORY* SUPPORT THE LEADERSHIP CHALLENGE CONCEPT?

The *LPI: Leadership Practices Inventory* is one of the best-selling and most trusted 360-degree leadership assessments available on the market. The instrument approaches leadership as a measurable, learnable, and teachable set of behaviors. This leadership assessment helps individuals and organizations measure their leadership competencies by providing a structured means of collecting and processing data based on The Five Practices.

Research shows that gathering 360-degree feedback is the first important step to improving performance and making behavior changes over time. The ratings are collected anonymously, with the exception of supervisor ratings, since most people have only one boss. The assessment of strengths and development needs is more reliable and valid because the individual receives input from multiple raters: him- or herself, supervisors, peers, direct reports, and others. Personal biases are significantly decreased by collecting feedback from individuals who have different relationships with the individual. Based on the collected data, the LPI delivers in-depth results with a detailed feedback report for each participant.

It is essential that the feedback report and scoring results be shared with the individual in a one-to-one or group setting that is led by a facilitator. The facilitator can assist individuals to:

- Make sense of the data and not become overwhelmed.
- Recognize the value and significance of the feedback and that their behavioral changes could make a difference.
- Trust that the feedback is both valid (it makes sense and results can be predicted based on other data) and reliable (statements are correlated and re-test results would be similar).
- Plan for the next steps.

The LPI Online has the ability to save data for future use so that leaders can compare their scores over multiple administrations. Taking this action is highly encouraged.

Once individuals receive their feedback, they are ready for tools, techniques, and knowledge to begin to make changes and increase the frequency of behaviors identified on the LPI. The LPI helps individuals to discover their leadership potential by providing them with the skills to master The Five Practices. Individuals can improve their skills by working on their own, attending additional LPI training sessions, or working with a coach.

If participants are working on their own, they may wish to use two particular tools included with their LPI 360. One of the tools is a set of user-friendly *LPI Participant Handouts* that takes participants to the heart and soul of their feedback results. A second tool is the *Leadership Development Planner* that was created to use over several months of coaching sessions. There are also numerous books, such as *The*

Leadership Challenge, Encouraging the Heart, A Leader's Legacy, The Leadership Challenge Workbook, and *Credibility,* that will enhance knowledge.

If you are a facilitator or a coach, there is a product for you to help leaders too, The Leadership Challenge® Facilitation Set which includes guidance for more than forty hours of workshops and more than one hundred experiential learning activities.

HOW TO USE THIS BOOK

In addition to the suggestions above, coaches using the LPI can turn to the rest of the chapters in this book for support. The book is divided into two distinct parts. Part I, Coaching to Improve The Five Practices, is written for experienced coaches who have their own coaching processes and are looking for ideas (questions, activities, books, or other resources) they can use with clients who have completed the LPI. Chapters 2 through 6 supply dozens of ideas to help your leader improve and increase the frequency of the behaviors that support The Five Practices.

Each chapter represents one of The Five Practices. It begins with a brief review of the practice, its two commitments, and its four essentials. Each of the six items in the LPI that relate to the chapter's practice are listed (items are numbered and listed in the order as they appear in the LPI to make it easy to locate). You, the coach, will determine which items to address based on your client's Feedback Report.

After each LPI item, you will find suggestions for:

- Questions you can ask your clients to initiate discussion or to delve into their philosophy about the practice and/or the LPI item.
- Activities created for a coaching situation. There are many more activities than you would ever use with one person. Work with your client to identify one that will be most useful. Even better, have your clients create their own after you present some possibilities.

At the end of each chapter we provide:

- A resource list that includes books, articles, websites, and blogs, if available, for you or your client to use.
- A section titled "How the Coach Models This Practice," which serves as a reminder about what you must do to be a positive, proactive model for your client.

Remember, the value of these activities and discussion questions is not in the doing, but in the follow-on discussion with you, the coach. Be sure to allow time to discuss the "so what" and the "now what" that occur as a result of any discussion or activity.

Part II, Improve Your Coaching Competence, provides an overview of coaching. It is written for someone who is familiar with The Leadership Challenge® Model, but wants to learn more about coaching. Chapter 7 presents an overview of coaching, and Chapter 8 allows coaches, new as well as experienced, to assess their coaching skills and to add knowledge and ideas for how to improve their skills. Chapter 9 lays out a coaching process that will show you how to take your leader from feedback to success. Chapter 10 addresses what to do when things go wrong, and Chapter 11 helps you coach yourself to greater heights by providing ideas to improve your skills as a coach as well as knowledge about The Leadership Challenge® Model.

Coaching leaders is a noble task. The only thing this world needs more than excellent leaders is excellent coaches to rally, inspire, and accompany them on their journeys.

CHAPTER 2: COACHING TO MODEL THE WAY

In This Chapter

- Review the Model the Way practice.
- List the corresponding commitments.
- Identify the six LPI items that reference this practice.
- Examine potential questions and activities a coach could use.
- Provide additional resources.
- Consider how the coach could model this practice.

Exemplary leaders know that if they want to gain commitment and achieve the highest standards, they must be models of the behavior they expect of others. It all begins with leaders who effectively Model the Way. To model the behavior they expect of others, leaders must first be clear about their guiding principles. But leaders are not just representing themselves. They speak and act on behalf of their teams and a larger organization and must forge agreement around common principles and common values. Leaders set the example through their daily actions that demonstrate that they are committed to their beliefs. Exemplary leaders Clarify Values and Set the Example by aligning their actions with shared values.

CLARIFY VALUES

One quality of admired leaders stands out above all else: They have strong beliefs about matters of principle. They have, or had, an unwavering commitment to a clear set of values. They are, or were, passionate about their causes. People expect their leaders to speak out on matters of values and conscience. But to speak out, leaders have to know what to speak about. To stand up for their beliefs, they have to know what they stand for. To walk the talk, leaders have to have a talk to walk. To do what they say, they have to know what they want to say. To earn and sustain personal credibility, leaders must first be able to clearly articulate deeply held beliefs.

That is why Clarify Values is the first of the leader commitments. It is where it all begins. To become credible, leaders must first comprehend fully the deeply held beliefs—values, principles, standards, ethics, and ideals—that drive them. Leaders must choose the principles they will use to guide their decisions and actions and then genuinely express them. To Clarify Values, a leader must engage in these two essentials:

- Find his or her voice
- Affirm shared values

Find his or her voice. Values influence every aspect of our lives: moral judgments, responses to others, as well as commitments to personal and organizational goals. Values set parameters for the decisions we make every day. Values also serve as guides to action, informing us when to say yes and when to say no. Values are empowering and motivating, keeping us focused on why we are doing what we are doing. Once leaders have identified their values, they need to give voice to those values—express them in their own way. Just as a leader cannot lead out of someone else's experience, he or she cannot lead through someone else's values and words. Leaders have a responsibility to be conscious of the words they choose because these words send signals about how leaders view the world.

Affirm shared values. Shared values form the foundation for building productive and genuine working relationships. Leaders build on agreement. They don't try to get everyone to be in accord on everything, because a leader does encourage diversity. However, recognition of shared values provides people with a common language, and tremendous energy is generated when individual, group, and organizational values are in synch. Commitment, enthusiasm, and drive are intensified. People have reasons to care about their work; they become more effective and satisfied and experience less stress. Employees are more loyal when they believe that their values are aligned with those of the organization. A unified voice on values results from discovery and dialogue. So although leaders' being clear on their values is essential, it is insufficient alone. There must be agreement on the shared values that everyone will commit to uphold.

SET THE EXAMPLE

Leaders take every opportunity to show others by their own example that they are deeply committed to the values and aspirations they espouse. No one will believe leaders are serious until they see them doing what they ask of others. Leading by example makes visions and values tangible to others. This is the evidence that leaders are personally committed. Set the Example is all about execution. It is about practicing what a leader preaches. It is about following through on commitments and keeping promises.

Leaders can become the role models for what the whole team represents. They also create a culture in which everyone commits to aligning with shared values. There are two essentials necessary to Set the Example, one that's focused on the leader and one that's focused on the constituents. To Set the Example, a leader needs to:

- Personify the shared values
- Teach others to model the values

Personify the shared values. Every action a leader completes sends a signal. Each action affords the chance to show where a leaders stands on matters of principle. Exemplary leaders are mindful of the signals they send and how they send them. The clearest indicator of what is important to leaders is how they spend their time. Leaders who spend their time on the most important values send a strong message. Leaders also personify shared values through their language, using words that best express the culture they want to create. When leaders ask purposeful questions, they intentionally stimulate people to think more purposefully about values. Finally, leaders seek feedback. They ask about the impact of their behavior on others and value the feedback they receive. Each of these actions sends signals about how deeply leaders respect and represent their espoused values.

Teach others to model the values. It is not just the leader who is watched, but everyone else on the team as well. Therefore it behooves leaders to ensure that everyone's actions are aligned with shared values. How can they do this? At least three key actions exist. First, leaders can confront critical incidents. They can respond to any disruptive occurrences. These critical incidents present opportunities for leaders to teach important lessons about appropriate behavior norms. Second, leaders can tell stories. When leaders publicly give examples of what team members

17

do to live the values, they have an opportunity to use the "moral of the story" to help others understand how to model the values. And finally, leaders can reinforce any behaviors they want repeated. They can track and measure performance to determine consistency with the values and recognize, both tangibly and intangibly, the performance consistent with espoused values.

Model the Way means that the leader has stated what values are important; has, by example, aligned those values to actions; and has invited the team to share the same values. Leaders can begin this important work with a personal audit of how they spend their time, how they communicate, how they ask questions, and how they use storytelling. To summarize, Model the Way incorporates two commitments.

- **Commitment 1:** Clarify values by finding your voice and affirming shared values.
- **Commitment 2:** Set the example by aligning actions with shared values.

Model the Way is about earning the right and the respect to lead through direct involvement and action. People follow first the person, then the plan.

MODEL THE WAY: PRACTICE FOR THE LPI ITEMS

The following six statements refer to the items in the *LPI: Leadership Practices Inventory* that relate to the Model the Way Practice. The numbers reference the item number in the LPI. These items are numbered and listed in the order as they appear in the LPI. This is done to make it easy to locate each item in this book; the order in which the items are discussed in this book does not suggest an order of importance. You need to determine, based on your client's feedback, which items your client wants to work on and in what sequence.

After each item you will find suggested questions and activities. These are created for a coaching situation and may be used with the leader(s) you may be coaching. Several of the activities reference a "journal." There is an assumption that your leader will have a personal journal in which to track plans, questions, and desires. A journal is an important tool for reflection on a leader's journey to excellence.

Note: There are many more activities than you would ever use with one person. Work with your client to identify one that will be most useful. Even better, have your clients create their own after you present some possibilities. Remember, the value of these activities and discussion questions is not in the doing, but in the follow-on discussion with you, the coach. Be sure to allow time to discuss the "so what" and the "now what" that occur as a result of any discussion or activity.

At the end of this chapter you will also find a resource list that includes books, articles, websites, and blogs for you or your client to use. You will also find a section titled "How the Coach Models This Practice," which serves as a reminder to you about what you must do to be a positive, proactive model for your client.

1. I set a personal example of what I expect of others.

Questions You Can Ask

- What do you think it means to "set a personal example"?
- What are your top three defining values?
- Imagine that you are setting the perfect personal example; what would it look like?
- How will you know what the expectations are?
- What do you wish leaders you've worked for in the past had done more? Less?
- Who can you relate to who sets a good personal example?
- Where do you think there might be a disconnect between what you say and what you do?
- Why should someone want to follow you?
- If your team could select its leader, would they choose you? Why do you think that?

Activities You Can Suggest

- **Squeaky Clean Model:** As a leader you must model the utmost integrity and professionalism. Tempted to pad your last expense report? Don't do it. Laughed at the last off-color joke? Don't do it. Smiled when someone used a stereotypical comment? Don't do it. Told a white lie about why you forgot to do something? Don't do it. The harm is not in each of the little things that may have tempted you. The harm is in fooling yourself that it's okay. You need to model the highest level of integrity and professionalism for your team members. Setting an example is the most powerful act a leader can do. Besides, you have to live with yourself. This is an excellent topic for you to track in your journal.

- **Quote to Ponder:** Michelangelo said, "Trifles make perfection, and perfection is no trifle." What does this mean to you? How do you translate this to your daily work, your philosophy, and the business you are in? What are the trifles that you deal with? How do these trifles lead to perfection? Which trifles do you need in order to set a personal example? How do you plan to do that? Make an entry in your journal. Remind yourself to review the answers to these questions next week after you've slept on it for a few days.

- **Be from Missouri:** As a leader you must lead by example. You influence your employees' thoughts and behaviors—probably more than you think. Regardless of what appears in your job description or in employee handbooks, your behavior is the real performance standard your employees and team members will emulate. They will assume it is okay and appropriate to do whatever they see you do. This means that it is critical that you set the example. You need to model the behavior and performance you expect from others. There's no magic here. It's really quite simple—just pretend that you are from Missouri—the "show-me state." Whether it is attitude, attendance, work ethic, or respect for others, simply show your team members what you expect them to do. Identify areas for which you may not be the model that you would like your team members to follow. Then decide what you will do differently. At a future time you may wish to discuss your planned changes with your supervisor.

- **Questions:** For each of your core values, write three questions you can ask that will create discussions about the value.

- **Audit Your Time:** At the end of a typical week, using your paper or electronic calendar, complete an audit of how you spent your time. Ask yourself, "If someone were to look at my calendar and demand evidence that I am demonstrating in my everyday actions that what I say is important, would he or she find it? Are my espoused values showing up in what I do every day?"

- **Create Your Story:** Many people in an organization have a story about what the organization has done for them. Create your own story and be prepared to tell it to others in and outside the business.

- **Define it:** Meet with your supervisor or another key individual in your organization and ask him or her to define what it means to Model the Way. Ask for ideas for how this could occur naturally in the day-to-day work arena. Take good notes.

- **Review The Five Practices:** Schedule a series of five weekly meetings with your supervisor. Ask him or her to dedicate each meeting to one or two of the practices. During this time, create a discussion. Questions might include:
  - What does this practice mean to you?
  - What should I be doing on a day-to-day basis to model this particular practice?
  - Can you provide me with some examples of what to avoid?
  - What tips do you have for ensuring that my direct reports also live this practice?
  - What feedback do you have for how I could do better in living according to this practice?
- **Role Model:** Be a role model for your values, even when you are not on the job. That's the meaning of integrity—being the same person regardless of the setting. This benefits both you and the organization. Note the reasons why in your journal.
- **Be Your Personal Best:** The name Vince Lombardi communicates such strong visions of excellence, discipline, commitment and, of course, winning. Even after his death in 1970, his famous speech, "What It Takes to Be Number 1," has continued to inspire and motivate countless people. The Lombardi philosophy transcends football. His powerful words capture the fundamentals of success—in any sport, any business, or in any life. Track down a recording or video clip of the speech. What is the message here for you? How does this thinking support your ability to set a personal example? How does it drive the business? How does it help you with all five practices?

6. I make certain that people adhere to the principles and standards that have been agreed upon.

Questions You Can Ask

- How do you interpret this practice? This item?
- How do you think your employees may have interpreted this question?
- How are you currently modeling this behavior?
- What do you think you need to do to shore it up?
- What's not being said that needs to be said?

- If "ensuring that your people adhered to the principles and standards" was a service or product you were selling, what would you do to make it a best-seller?
- Why do you believe this is an important skill?
- Which principles and standards are people not living up to? Why is that?

Activities You Can Suggest

- **Speak Up:** When you see or hear someone who is not adhering to the standards, speak up. As a leader, you are obligated to not only live the vision and values, but to ensure that other do. Think back to times when individuals were not living the vision and values and you did not speak up. Perhaps you even chuckled at an inappropriate joke, nodded your head in agreement about a stereotype comment. Why didn't you speak up? Were you embarrassed? Uncomfortable? Thought it wasn't your job? Just didn't think about it? Remember, if you want your people to live the vision most of the time, you need to live the vision *all* of the time. In the same vein, be sure to speak up when you see someone doing something well. Reinforce him or her. Corrections, though, should be made in private.
- **Hold Yourself Accountable:** Holding others accountable means that you hold yourself accountable first. Take one specific week to work on just this skill. At the end of each day, use your scheduler or your to-do notes to remind yourself of what you did. Create four columns on a page of paper. List your tasks, meetings, and phone calls in the first column. In the second column, write down all the things that you did that adhered to the standards. In the third column, write all the things that you could have added or done more/better with regard to the standards. In the fourth column, note any opportunities that arose where you could have done a better job of holding others accountable. They may be small things, such as someone who interrupted someone else and you did not make an attempt to correct the behavior. Understanding your own behavior makes you more aware of opportunities to hold others accountable for adhering to the standards. Take this activity one step further. Share it with your employees and ask them to repeat the same thing you did. Meet with each of them to learn about their results.
- **Standards Review:** Meet with your direct reports. Ask them to review the agreed-on standards with you. Ask these questions to start the discussion:
  - What do our standards mean to you?
  - What part of the standards do you need to understand better?

- How do you model the standards throughout the day?
- What makes it easy or difficult to adhere to the standards?
- How can I help you adhere to the standards more easily?
- **Reward Adhering to the Standards:** Encourage team members to reinforce other team members when they see them adhering to the standards and modeling appropriately. If possible, post their kudos on a central bulletin board.
- **Create Legends:** Identify one of more people in your organization who are modeling the shared values. Tell stories in meetings and other events about what they are doing to set the example for others.
- **Today Versus Tomorrow:** Focusing on today's standards while maintaining focus on the vision and long-term goals is critical for a leader, but not easy to do. Meet with your supervisor to discuss this dilemma. You might start with these questions.
  - How do I anticipate and plan for the worst- and best-case scenarios?
  - How do I consider the potential consequences for all stakeholders?
  - How accurately have I predicted and assessed potential risks and benefits this year?
  - How well do I hold others accountable for adhering to the standards while achieving short-term goals?
  - How well do I relate my direct reports' goals and standards to living the vision?
  - What have you noticed that I could do better to help my employees adhere to our standards?
  - How can I improve my performance in these areas?

11. I follow through on promises and commitments that I make.

Questions You Can Ask

- How do you interpret this practice?
- What gets in your way of following through on promises and commitments?
- How do you think your friends and family would rate you on this behavior? Does your response give you any clues about what might be happening at work?
- What if you had scored the highest on this behavior? What would be different?
- Can you tell me about a time when this behavior was not a problem for you?

- What's enjoyable about following through on promises and commitments?
- What's uncomfortable about not following through on promises and commitments?
- What's uncomfortable about following through on promises and commitments?
- How has this behavior created concerns for your employees?

Activities You Can Suggest

- **Do Some Personal Soul-Searching:** Start a new section in your journal. Do a personal check on the things that have a deeper meaning to you. Getting in touch with who you are makes it easier to hold yourself and others accountable. Here are a few questions that you might explore personally. Search your soul for the answers.
  - What makes you laugh?
  - What makes you cry?
  - What gives you energy?
  - What makes you angry?
  - What's your dream for your future?
  - What have you allowed to prevent you from being who you are? Does this relate in any way to your follow-through?
  - What roles do you play in life (father, brother, leader, etc.)? Are you balancing all roles? What roles would you like to increase? Decrease? Remain the same?
  - How well do you think you follow through on promises and commitments at home? With your family? With friends?
  - How well do you think you are following through on promises and commitments at work? Are you satisfied with your performance? Who could you ask for confirmation?
- **360-Degree Review:** You are most likely focusing on this skill within this practice because of the feedback you received on your LPI. List what you have done to improve in this area: "Follows through on promises and commitments." Schedule an appointment with your supervisor and/or coach and tell him or her what you have done to improve your skills and knowledge. Ask the following questions:
  - What changes have you noticed?
  - Can you give me some examples of times when I could have done something better?

- What changes in my behavior and performance do you suggest I address next?
- What advice do you have for me?
- **Take Note:** Carry a pocket notebook with you for the next week. Every time you speak with someone, get in the habit of taking the notebook out of your pocket and writing a short note about what you discussed. If you said you would do something, put a star next to the item. At the end of each day, review your notes. Identify promises and commitments and whether you kept them or not. Check off any you completed. Make a mental note—or add to your to-do list—any items that you still need to complete.
- **Use Your Mobile Device:** List any commitments or promises to others on your mobile device or other calendar/scheduling source. Check daily and weekly to ensure you are living up to your commitments.
- **Daily Checkup:** At the end of each day, ask yourself these three questions: How did I demonstrate today that I am committed to the principles that I espouse? How did I act in ways that were inconsistent with the principles that I espouse? What can I do tomorrow to make sure that I am consistent in word and deed?

16. I ask for feedback on how my actions affect other people's performance.

Questions You Can Ask

- How do you interpret this behavior?
- When do you think this is the biggest problem? The least problem?
- How often does your supervisor ask for feedback on how his or her actions affect your behavior? How does that make you feel?
- What do you need to do to improve this behavior?
- Whose performance do you think your actions affect and how?
- What if you started asking for feedback that would change the situation? Who would you ask? How often? Under what circumstances? What specifically might you say? What do you think the response would be?
- What is within your power to make this change?

Activities You Can Suggest

- **How Well Am I Doing?** Schedule a meeting with your supervisor to discuss whether he or she believes you are modeling the organization's vision, values, goals, and strategy through your actions and performance. Use the following questions to start the discussion. Ask your supervisor to rate you on a 1 to 7 scale with 7 being very good and 1 being poor.
    - How well do my actions align with the organization's goals and strategies?
    - How well does my performance align with the vision?
    - How well does my performance align with the values?
    - How well do I strengthen customer relationships?
    - How do my actions affect others' performance?
    - How well do I reinforce what we stand for—Model the Way?
    - How well do I demonstrate my personal commitment to team members?
  Actions that address these questions help to ensure that you create an environment that inspires team members and gets the job done. You may also want to ask your peers these same questions to determine whether everyone sees what you are doing in the same way.
- **Mistakes Are a Gift:** Teddy Roosevelt stated, "He who makes no mistakes, makes no progress." Observe how you react to mistakes. If you think about it, the times that you learned the most were the times when you made a mistake. Do you admit to your mistakes? Do you apologize when appropriate? Are you defensive? Ask a trusted friend's opinion as well. If you react badly or make no mistakes at all, you may be considered as "unteachable" to those above you. Take on a perspective of being a life-long learner. Make mistakes. Accept the feedback. Apologize when appropriate. Learn from your mistakes.
- **Do Something:** Listen to the feedback you receive today. We all receive feedback every day. Pay attention for twenty-four hours. Who did you receive it from? How did you react? Have you heard this before? Finally, do something! Accept the feedback. Make the change. Develop yourself.
- **Ask for It!** Ask your supervisor, co-workers, peers, and your subordinates for ideas to develop your leadership skills and knowledge. Ask specifically about your interactions with others and how they might affect others' performance. In addition, ask for suggestions for how you could practice some of these skills or learn some of the information. Establish goals based on the input and create or modify your goals.

- **Feedback on Your Feedback:** Complete self-analysis instruments such as the *Myers-Briggs Type Indicator* (MBTI) or styles instruments such as the Everything DiSC®. After reviewing the results with your coach, obtain feedback on the results from a co-worker. How accurate does your co-worker think the measure was? What can you do to be more effective based on the feedback from your coach, the instrument, and your co-worker? How might your style affect your action and communication with others?

- **You Know It When You Want to:** We may not listen well when we don't want to hear the message. That may occur when you are receiving feedback—especially if you disagree with the message. Interestingly, one of the most important times to listen well is when you disagree with the message, especially as it relates to how we affect others. Identify other times when you may not listen as well as you should (when the message is boring, when you lack respect for the speaker, when you are tired, when you have too much to do). Create your own personal action plan to improve your listening skills at all times and for all situations. Listening is seen as one of the most important leadership skills. How well you listen has a major impact on your job effectiveness and on the quality of your relationships with others. You listen to obtain information. You listen to understand. You listen for enjoyment. You listen to learn. Go to www.mindtools.com/CommSkll/ActiveListening.htm to pick up a few tips about how to be a better listener. Take notes and implement immediately.

21. I build consensus around a common set of values for running our organization.

Questions You Can Ask

- How do you define consensus?
- Who is involved in establishing the consensus of values?
- What does your set of values state? Who knows about them?
- How much time/energy would it take to establish a set of values for your department?
- What would change if you had a common set of values?
- What's possible for the future with consensus around the values?
- Why do you think this is important to the people who completed your LPI?

Activities You Can Suggest

- **Values Meetings:** Schedule a series of values meetings with your direct reports. Dedicate each meeting to one or two values. Have team members bring either objects or stories that represents the value to them. You should begin the first couple of discussions yourself to help them feel comfortable about sharing their stories.

- **Our History:** Build consensus around the values by determining where they originated. Identify someone who can share the history of the organization with your team. How did the culture begin? Culture is built through the years as leaders develop it. Corporate culture doesn't just happen; it is developed purposefully. Usually a company's culture can be traced back to the founders' views of what the organization should be and what it should represent. Eventually the beliefs regarding employees, customers, competitors, quality, and service are woven together to become a part of the fabric that is the culture of the organization. The culture and values are related in that the culture is the past through the present and the values represent both the past and the present. Ask your team members how they support the values.

- **Strategic Decision Review:** Discuss this as a team. Think about a strategic challenge or decision your team recently faced. Consider possible situations that had either or both long-term impact and far-reaching results.
  - How well did the team practice strategic thinking as it relates to the situation and the organizational vision? Did anyone verbalize the values during the decision making?
  - How did the values play a role in the final decision?
  - As you think about the final result, is there any information that you wish you had, but did not? What prevented you from having that data?
  - How open and candid was the decision-making process? What hidden agendas existed?
  - When you consider the final decision, how aligned is it to the organizational values and vision?

- **Building Consensus:** Building consensus around the organization's values is an important part of being able to Model the Way. Bring your team together. Begin by presenting your personal value statement. Value statements define how people want to behave with each other in their personal and professional lives. Share the values that are most important to you, the values you believe in and that define your character. Then ask team members to share their value statements. Encourage questions and discussion. Build consensus about those values that are the most important to everyone.

- **My Values in the Organization:** Share your value statement with your supervisor. Ask him or her to compare your values to those of the organization. Is there compatibility? Are there gaps? State how you see your values as giving you the ability to strive to do your best. Ask your supervisor for thoughts and opinions about what you have stated. Meet with your direct reports as a group. Share your supervisor's comments with them. Create a discussion and reach consensus about what everyone needs to do to reach a common set of values for the team and the organization.

26. I am clear about my philosophy of leadership.

Questions You Can Ask

- How do you interpret this practice?
- What are your top three defining values?
- As a leader, how would you most like to be remembered?
- Imagine it is five years from now. What leadership legacy have you created?
- How do you describe your leadership philosophy?
- How would your employees know what your leadership philosophy states?
- To what degree is a leadership philosophy an expectation in your organization?
- How would your day-to-day work change if everyone in your department knew exactly how to define your leadership philosophy?
- What's preventing you from clarifying your leadership philosophy?
- What would make this task easier, more fun, or more meaningful to you?
- What are the benefits of sharing your leadership philosophy? The drawbacks?

Activities You Can Suggest

- **Top Ten Best Actors:** The top ten actors with the most Oscar nominations are Jack Nicholson (12), Laurence Olivier (10), Paul Newman and Spencer Tracy (9), Marlon Brando, Jack Lemmon, and Al Pacino (8), Richard Burton, Dustin Hoffman, and Peter O'Toole (7). You can be sure that each of them strives to be the best in every movie. Share this trivia with one or two others you work with. Then discuss what it means to strive to be the best. How do you think they do that? Why? How is what they do as actors similar to what you do at work? How is an actor's philosophy similar to a leader's philosophy? What is the payoff for anyone who strives to be the best? All of you can learn from each other. Share how you determined your leadership philosophy. What ideas did you take away from this exercise? How did it help clarify your leadership philosophy?

- **Personal Values:** Clarity about your personal values is important to establish the foundation of your philosophy. Take time to note a few of your personal values. They could include things such as "I respect everyone's right to be who he wants to be," or "I value loyalty, candor, creativity, and the willingness to continue to learn." It doesn't have to be a long statement, but it has to be a *you*-statement. The following are examples of values you might use as the starting point for articulating your values:

    ambition, competence, individuality, equality, integrity, service, responsibility, accuracy, respect, dedication, diversity, improvement, enjoyment, loyalty, credibility, honesty, innovativeness, teamwork, excellence, accountability, empowerment, quality, efficiency, dignity, collaboration, stewardship, empathy, accomplishment, courage, wisdom, independence, security, challenge, influence, learning, compassion, friendliness, discipline, generosity, persistency, optimism, dependability, flexibility.

Value statements define how people want to behave with each other in their personal and professional lives. Choose the values that are most important to you, the values you believe in and that define your character. Then live them visibly every day at work and at home. Living your values is one of the most powerful tools available to help you be an excellent leader.

Conduct this same exercise with your employees. Then build consensus about those that are the most important to everyone.

Note: The Leadership Challenge Values Cards are a useful tool to consider using when doing this exercise. They are a deck of fifty-two cards with values words like the ones above printed directly on the cards. They come with instructions on how to use them for personal values clarification as well as in group settings. They are available for purchase at www.leadershipchallenge.com.

- **My Values, Your Values, and the Organization:** *Part I*. Your values are made up of everything that has happened to you in your life and include influences from your parents and family, your religious affiliation, your friends and peers, your education, your reading, and more. Effective people recognize these environmental influences and identify and develop a clear, concise, and meaningful set of values and priorities. Once defined, values impact every aspect of your life. You demonstrate and model your values in action in your personal and work behaviors, decision making, contribution, and interpersonal interaction. Share your value statement with your supervisor. Ask him or her to compare your values to those of the organization. Is there compatibility? Are there gaps? State how you see your values as giving you the ability to strive to do your best. Ask your supervisor for thoughts and opinions about what you have stated. Thank your supervisor for his or her time and state that you would like to think about what the two of you have discussed and that you would like to revisit this discussion in a week or two. Spend time over the next week considering the discussion and your next steps.

Part II. Repeat the above steps with your employees. Meet with them individually and as a group.

- **Be True to Yourself:** Leaders who are credible to others are authentic—those who are true to themselves but steeped in the principles that guide them. They recognize that, while they may be in charge, principles ultimately govern. Building character and culture is a function of aligning your beliefs and behaviors with principles that are external, objective, and self-evident. They operate regardless of your awareness of them. What principles guide an authentic leader? Authentic leaders are humble. They are unassuming in the way that they share the glory with their team members and are modest about their accomplishments. Their courage ensures that they have the integrity to make the right choices when necessary. Skills that will help you become more authentic include:
  - Self-awareness enables you to understand yourself. Keeping a journal will assist you with this.
  - Independence enables you to make the changes that are necessary, to stand up for yourself and what you know is right.
  - Creative thinking allows you to create beyond your present reality and enables you to set goals, plan for the future, and visualize yourself living your mission. As a leader you must accept the prerequisite of authenticity to Model the Way. Capture your thoughts in your journal. How well do you exhibit these authentic skills? Identify ways for addressing any difficulty in achieving the level of authenticity you desire. Ask others whom you admire about authenticity. How did they move toward being more authentic?

- **Be the Best:** These three little words are extremely powerful. Meet with your supervisor and reveal that you wish to improve in every way and to strive to be the best. Ask for ideas that display how you can be the best at all you can do. State that you would appreciate it if your supervisor would carry a "best card" (an index card) with him or her for the next week and write down everything that your supervisor thinks needs improvement so that you can be the best. Then schedule a "best" meeting with him or her in a week to hear all the ideas that were generated during the week.
- **Leader Legacy:** Interview your supervisor and another leader separately. Ask them what they intend to leave behind as a leadership legacy. Take notes. Compare the two. Now create your own leadership legacy. What leadership legacy do you want to leave to others? What do you want others to say about your leadership after you've left your current position or the organization? What lasting impact do you want to have on the organization? What impact do you want to have on the people? Write it in your journal.
- **Brand You:** Organizations brand themselves, their products, and, most recently, their leadership styles. You can do the same. You can brand your leadership style to set the stage for what you stand for and how you can set an example and Model the Way. Work with a co-worker to complete this activity so that you can each be a sounding board for the other. Develop these six aspects of your personal leadership brand.
  1. *Reputation:* Building your leadership brand is like developing a reputation. What do you want to be known for? What is your area of expertise? What qualities and skills make you unique?
  2. *Values:* What do you stand for? What do you believe in? What values should guide your decisions and actions? Your brand has to have integrity, and that means *you* must have integrity. Being consistent with your values is one of the most important ways your personal brand builds its integrity.
  3. *Vision:* Your leadership brand must have a solid vision. What is your desired leadership future? Work through mental scenarios and define the outcome and the emotion attached to that outcome. The most satisfied people are those whose visions are congruent with their organization's vision.
  4. *Presence:* Being present, or your ability to remain in a state of wholeness at any time, is a basic leadership skill. Practice presence by focusing your attention and practicing authenticity.

5. *Trustworthiness:* Any brand that you purchase carries with it a certain amount of trust, a promise of quality and satisfaction. You must earn trust. How can you do that? Do what you say you will do (DWYSYWD). Be honest and candid. Be supportive. Let people in on who you are.

6. *Learn:* A brand rarely sits idle without continuous improvement. Neither shall leaders. Learn and grow intentionally, becoming better and wiser with every experience.

Work through each of the six aspects deciding: How do I define this? How do I evaluate myself in this area? What can I do to make improvements? How will I know I have improved? What is my leadership brand?

- **Align Personal Values:** What are your values? Compare your values with the organization's values. Are they congruent? If not, why not? Use this information to clarify your leadership philosophy.

BOOKS, ARTICLES, AND WEBSITES TO RECOMMEND

Books for Model the Way

- David M. Armstrong. *Managing by Storying Around: A New Method of Leadership.* New York: Doubleday, 1992.
- Warren Bennis, Daniel Goleman, and James O'Toole. *Transparency: How Leaders Create a Culture of Candor.* San Francisco: Jossey-Bass, 2008.
- Peter Block. *The Answer to How Is Yes: Acting on What Matters.* San Francisco: Berrett-Koehler, 2002.
- Po Bronson. *What Should I Do with My Life? The True Story of People Who Answered the Ultimate Question.* New York: Random House, 2001.
- Steven R. Covey. *The Seven Habits of Highly Effective People.* New York: Simon & Schuster, 2004.
- Max De Pree. *Leadership Is an Art.* New York: Doubleday, 2004.
- Marshall Goldsmith. *What Got You Here Won't Get You There: How Successful People Become Even More Successful.* New York: Hyperion, 2011.
- Robert K. Greenleaf. *Servant Leadership: A Journey into Legitimate Power and Greatness.* New York: Paulist Press, 2002.

- James M. Kouzes and Barry Z. Posner. *Credibility: How Leaders Gain and Lose It, Why People Demand It*. San Francisco: Jossey-Bass, 2003.
- David H. Maister. *Practice What You Preach: What Managers Must Do to Create a High Achievement Culture*. New York: The Free Press, 2001.
- Parker J. Palmer. *Let Your Life Speak: Listening to the Voice of Vocation*. San Francisco: Jossey-Bass, 2000.
- Terry Pearce. *Leading Out Loud: The Authentic Speaker, The Credible Leader*. San Francisco: Jossey-Bass, 1995.
- Tony Simons. *The Integrity Dividend: Leading by the Power of Your Word*. San Francisco: Jossey-Bass, 2008.
- Craig Wortmann. *What's Your Story? Using Stories to Ignite Performance and Be More Successful*. Chicago: Kaplan Publishing, 2006.

Articles

- "A Leader's Framework for Decision Making," *Harvard Business Review,* November 2007. Wise executives tailor their approach to fit the complexity of the circumstances they face.
- "Building a Leadership Brand," *Harvard Business Review,* July 2007. You want your leaders to be the kind of people who embody the promises your company makes to its customers. To build this capability, follow these five principles.
- "The Secrets to Successful Strategy Execution," *Harvard Business Review,* June 2008. Research shows that organizations fail at executing strategy to drive the business because they neglect the most powerful drivers of effectiveness: decision responsibility and information flow.
- "Mastering the Management System," *Harvard Business Review,* January 2008. Successful strategy execution has two basic rules: understand the management cycle that links strategy and operations, and know what tools to apply at each stage of the cycle.
- "The Ethical Mind: A Conversation with Psychologist Howard Gardner," *Harvard Business Review,* March 2007. It's not enough to espouse high standards. To live up to them—and help others do the same—requires an ethical cast of mind that lets you practice your principles consistently.
- "The Seasoned Executive's Decision-Making Style," *Harvard Business Review,* February 2006. New research shows that senior managers analyze and act on

problems far differently than their more junior co-workers do. Those whose thinking does not evolve may not advance.

- "What Leaders Really Do," *Harvard Business Review,* December 2001. They don't make plans; they don't solve problems; they don't even organize people. What leaders really do is prepare organizations for change and help them cope as they struggle through it.
- "Discovering Your Authentic Leadership," *Harvard Business Review,* February 2007. We all have the capacity to inspire and empower others. But we must first be willing to devote ourselves to our personal growth and development as leaders.

Websites/Blogs

- www.managementhelp.org. The library provides easy access to 650 topics spanning five thousand links regarding the leadership and management of yourself, other individuals, groups, and organizations.
- www.mindtools.com. Management, leadership, and career tools and hundreds of essential skill-builder articles free of charge. In addition, sign up for a free e-newsletter.

HOW THE COACH MODELS THIS PRACTICE

- ◆ Make sure that you have clarified your values before you ask your client/leader to do this. Be prepared to share your values with your leader as part of a dialogue on what's important to both of you.
- ◆ Model what you expect from your leader. If you expect your leader to be on time, you must be on time.
- ◆ If the leader does not adhere to something in your agreement, discuss it with him or her.
- ◆ Follow through on *all* commitments you make to the leader. If you say you will gather some information by a certain date, do so. In addition, be sure to commit to a specific date and time for all actions. This will model another aspect that is important for the leader.
- ◆ Ask for feedback from your leader at each meeting, for example: How did my suggestion work? How did this meeting go for you today?

- Reach consensus on your coaching agreement.
- Share a written copy of your personal values statement, leadership philosophy, guiding principles, whatever you have that demonstrates your underlying belief system.

CHAPTER 3: COACHING TO INSPIRE A SHARED VISION

In This Chapter

- Review the Inspire a Shared Vision practice.
- List the corresponding commitments.
- Identify the six LPI items that reference this practice.
- Examine potential questions and activities a coach could use.
- Provide additional resources.
- Consider how the coach could model this practice.

Exemplary leaders are forward-looking, able to envision the future and enlist others to support it. Leaders who Inspire a Shared Vision can gaze across the horizon of time and imagine the greater opportunities to come. They see something out ahead and are able to develop an ideal and unique image of the future for the common good. Although most of us have aspirations and dreams and want tomorrow to be better than today, successful leaders ensure that what they see is also something that others will see as well. Shared visions attract more people, sustain higher levels of motivation, and withstand more challenges than those that are singular. A leader who can Inspire a Shared Vision must first Envision the Future and then Enlist Others in a common vision.

ENVISION THE FUTURE

Leaders create a vivid vision of the future by imagining exciting and ennobling possibilities.

A leader's excitement and clarity of vision become an inspiration to others. To create the inspiration, the leader must paint a picture of the future for others. A coach may try to identify an analogy that will help them create the picture. This will provide engaging, passionate words that excite and electrify employees and move them to action.

Leaders develop the capacity to envision the future by mastering these two essentials:

- Imagine the possibilities
- Find a common purpose

Imagine the possibilities. Leaders are dreamers. Leaders are idealists. Leaders are possibility thinkers. It is usually difficult for leaders to describe where their visions come from, but when they do, it is more about a feeling, a sense, or a gut reaction. When leaders identify their visions, they work through a self-exploration process. The best vision comes when a leader engages in conscious introspection. Leaders can do four things: reflect on the past, attend to the present, prospect the future, and feel their passion. Looking to their past first affords leaders the opportunity to make sense of the world retrospectively and to extrapolate the future from it. Leaders who attend to the present take the time to review current data and notice how they relate to each other. Leaders generally do not spend enough time being forward-looking, but should because this is the only way that they can project themselves ahead in time. Finally, leaders must find their passion because what they envision for the future is really all about expressing their passion. It is all about what gets them up in the morning. Exemplary leaders have a passion for something other than their own fame and fortune. They care about making a difference in the world.

Find a common purpose. Leaders are expected to be forward-looking, but they aren't expected to impose their visions of the future on others. People do not want to just hear about the leader's vision, they also want to hear about their own aspirations. How can leaders find a common purpose? First they can determine what is meaningful to others. There is a deep desire within everyone to make a difference, and when leaders clearly communicate a shared vision, they ennoble those who work on its behalf. Leaders can also create a cause for commitment. This is important because when people are a part of something that raises them to higher levels of motivation and morality, they belong to something special. Finally, leaders can be forward-looking at all times, in particular during times of rapid change. The speed of change doesn't really make a difference, except that it requires more intense focus. People want to follow those who can see beyond today's problems and visualize a brighter tomorrow.

ENLIST OTHERS

A shared vision of the future is necessary, but insufficient to achieve extraordinary results. People don't follow leaders who are only mildly enthusiastic about something. They have to be wildly enthusiastic for followers to give it their all. Constituents expect their leaders to be inspiring and to be a major source of energy.

Whether leaders are trying to mobilize a crowd in an auditorium or one person in the office, to enlist others, leaders must improve their capacities to act on these two essentials:

- Appeal to common ideals
- Animate the vision

Appeal to common ideals. Visions are about ideals, about a strong desire to achieve something great. They are expressions of optimism. Exemplary leaders provide people with a sense of meaning and purpose from what they take on. Leaders who communicate visions talk to people about how they are going to make a difference in the world. Leaders can be more successful if they connect to what is meaningful to their constituents. What truly excites people is knowing that they are a part of something that can make a profound difference to the future of their families, friends, colleagues, customers, and communities. They want to know that what they are doing really matters. A leader must take pride in being unique in order to foster pride and boost self-esteem in others; no one wants to be connected to something that is just like everyone else—average. Finally, leaders will be most successful if they appeal to people's ideals, move their souls, and uplift their spirits. Leaders accomplish this by aligning their dreams with the people's dreams.

Animate the vision. Leaders must arouse others to join in a cause to move decisively and boldly forward. Leaders recognize that their enthusiasm and expressiveness are among their strongest allies in their efforts to generate commitment in their constituents. By using symbolic language, creating word images of the future, practicing a positive communication style, tapping into verbal and nonverbal expressiveness, and speaking from their hearts, they breathe life into a vision. Leaders with a deep passion, who have a commitment to their cause, are exciting. It is fun to be around someone who is excited about the magic that is possible. People want leaders who are upbeat, optimistic, and confident about the future. It is the only way to get people to want to struggle for shared aspirations.

Inspire a Shared Vision is the practice of creating a unique and ideal image of the future for the common good of the team. A leader must envision the preferred future and enlist others in the exciting dream by appealing to their aspirations. The exemplary leader establishes a vivid vision and enlists others in the vision by sharing how it can encompass others' interests. The leader articulates a picture of what the preferred future looks like. To summarize, Inspire a Shared Vision is defined by two commitments.

- **Commitment 3:** Envision the future by imagining exciting and ennobling possibilities.
- **Commitment 4:** Enlist others in a common vision by appealing to shared aspirations.

Inspiring a shared vision is how leaders connect others to what is most meaningful in the vision. They lift people to higher levels and reinforce that they can make a difference in the world, making others feel proud to be a part of something extraordinary.

INSPIRE A SHARED VISION: PRACTICE FOR THE LPI ITEMS

The following six statements refer to the items in the *LPI: Leadership Practices Inventory* that relate to Inspire a Shared Vision. The numbers reference the item number in the LPI. These items are numbered and listed in the order as they appear in the LPI. This is done to make it easy to locate each item in this book; the order in which the items are discussed in this book does not suggest an order of importance. You need to determine, based on your client's Feedback Report, which items your client wants to work on and in what sequence.

After each item, you will find suggested questions and activities. These are created for a coaching situation and may be used with the leader(s) you may be coaching. Several of the activities reference a "journal." There is an assumption that your leader will have a personal journal in which to track plans, questions, and desires. A journal is an important tool for reflection on a leader's journey to excellence.

Note: There are many more activities than you would ever use with one person. Work with your client to identify one that will be most useful. Even better, have your clients create their own after you present some possibilities. Remember, the value of these activities and discussion questions is not in the doing, but in the follow-on discussion with you, the coach. Be sure to allow time to discuss the "so what" and the "now what" that occur as a result of any discussion or activity.

At the end of this chapter you will find a resource list that includes books, articles, websites, and blogs for you or your client to use. You will also find a section titled "How the Coach Models This Practice," which serves as a reminder to you about what you must do to be a positive, proactive model for your client.

2. I talk about future trends that will influence how our work gets done.

Questions You Can Ask

- How do you interpret this item?
- When looking back at the key milestones in your life, what was the theme or mission that kept propelling you forward?
- If you were looking back at today from ten years into the future, what would you remember?
- How do you prepare yourself to be knowledgeable about future trends?
- If you could speak to anyone you desired about future trends and how they will influence your work, who would you speak to and what would you say?
- What is your biggest obstacle in learning about future trends? Where do you find them? Where else could you look?
- How do you think future trends are related to the principle, Inspire a Shared Vision? How important is it to know other trends?
- How do you stay on top of trends in your organization? Your industry? Technology? Culture? Business? The arts? Science? Politics?
- If you were the president of your company, what would you do to prepare for the future?
- What is the reaction of others when you are talking about future trends?

Activities You Can Suggest

- **Monitoring Squad:** Create a group of four to eight people in your unit. Assign each one a resource to read such as *The New York Times, Fast Company,* or others. Meet weekly for lunch to discuss the trends each of you sees in the economy and the industry. Begin to ask questions of each other such as:
  - Where is this leading?
  - What are the implications for our business?
  - What are the threats and opportunities in this market that impact our future success?
  - What is our competitive advantage under circumstances such as these?
  - How will this affect our customers? What will we be expected to do about it?
  - What actions might be necessary to achieve success in this industry given the current environment?
  - What strategic thrusts should we be prepared to make given today's economy?
- **Upward Information Flow:** Track information about trends in your area of the industry and the economy. Share this information upward with your boss as well as with your employees. For support and/or background for this activity, read "The Secrets to Successful Strategy Execution" (*Harvard Business Review,* June 2008). The article shows that the most important reason organizations fail at executing strategy is because they neglect information flow.
- **Predict the Future:** Ask team members to imagine the world ten years from now. What do they think the organization will need to do in order to stay competitive? Decide which ideas you might be able to implement now.
- **Google Says:** Use a search engine to learn the perceptions others have of your company. How does this help you understand the business better? What other ways can you monitor trends using your search engine? Share what you learn with your employees.
- **Visit a Bookstore:** Visit a bookstore that has a varied selection of magazines and newspapers. Here is a list you may want to review on a broad spectrum of issues. Newspapers you should systematically scan include *The New York Times, The Washington Post, The Wall Street Journal, The Miami Herald, The Chicago Tribune, The Los Angeles Times, The Christian Science Monitor,* and *The Times of London.* Magazines include *Vital Speeches of the Day, Across the Board, Fast Company, Wired, Time, U.S. News and World Report, Futures, The Forum for Applied Research and Public Policy, World Monitor, Atlantic, The Nation, Ms, Utne,*

and *Reader*. Page through several of these. What opportunities do you see for your organization? Report back to your supervisor about what you have learned from your research. Share your discussion with your employees.

- **It's Worth a Subscription:** Subscribe *to Fast Company*. This subscription will keep you on the cutting edge of what's new and changing and inspire you to plan for future changes in your organization. When you have finished reading each issue, pass it around the office to encourage others to talk about future trends. Ask your employees what they read that might influence the work you all do.

- **Trends Journal:** Start a trends journal, tracking information you gather about the industry from various sources: *The Wall Street Journal,* television, speeches, your local newspaper, business journals. Track statistics as well as narrative comments. After a month, schedule time with your supervisor to discuss what you have learned. Obtain his or her feedback. Invite your supervisor to a staff meeting and re-create your discussion for your employees. Encourage questions.

- **Attend Senior Leader Meetings:** Attend several senior leader meetings. Observe and take notes. List all the changes big and small. Discuss the plans for these changes with your supervisor. Ask about necessity, how the changes fit within the strategy, and risk-management strategies. Share what you can with your employees.

- **Be an Observer:** Be an observer about the changing business environment outside of work. Think about the new products you purchase. What are your friends and family discussing and buying? What changes do you see in advertising on television and in the newspaper? What are the implications for your organization and future evolutionary changes that may be required? Note some of your predictions in a journal and review them in six months. Invite your direct reports to do the same. Compare notes on a monthly basis.

7. I describe a compelling image of what our future could be like.

Questions You Can Ask

- How do you interpret this item?
- How would you like to change the world?
- How do you select the words to use to describe your image of the future?

- How would you describe the words that you use to share your image of the future: cool and realistic; hot and exciting; other?
- What words do you find compelling? What words do others find compelling? What makes them compelling for you and others?
- If someone were going to draw a picture of your vision, what would he or she see?
- If you wanted me to become excited about your vision, what would you tell me?
- How have you made a difference in your organization? In people's lives? In the world?
- Why should I buy into your vision?
- What if you wanted the President of the United States to buy into your vision? What would you tell him or her?

Activities You Can Suggest

- **Envision Your Vision:** If you haven't done so already, write your vision for the future for you personally, your department, or your work group. Consider it a starting point for discussions with your team members.
- **Rate Yourself:** Are you keeping your employees apprised of your image of the future? One of your most important jobs is to coach your team members and develop them into the leaders of tomorrow. Rate yourself on how well you are aligning your team members using the following questions:
  - Do my team members know what the primary mission and vision are for our organization?
  - Do my team members understand what our organizational goals and objectives are?
  - To what extent do I keep my team members informed about current organizational plans, milestones, and operating results?
  - Do my team members have any input as to what our department's goals will be? How committed are they to the attainment of those goals?
  - Do my team members know how these goals and milestones help to enact our shared vision?
  - Do my team members understand the relationship between our own department's goals and those of the total organization?
  - To what extent do my team members have a say in determining how to achieve our team's goals?
  - Do my team members understand the role they play in the attainment of our team's goals?

- Can my team members identify their three or four key responsibilities?
- To what extent is there agreement between me and my team members as to what results I expect from them?
- Do I involve my team members fully in decisions that relate to them and their work?
- Do my team members know what I feel passionate about?

- **Add Passion:** Do you use inspiring, passionate words when you speak about the organization's vision? Such as "Big Hairy Audacious Goals," commonly known as BHAGs (pronounced Be' hags) from Jim Collins' writing; "Excellence" from Tom Peters; or "Let's make a dent in the universe!" per Steve Jobs are all examples of such language. Review your word choice. Review your inspiration quotient. Review your enthusiasm. As a leader, would you inspire others to follow you where they wouldn't go alone? Would you follow you? If not, plan how you will stir up the passion.

- **How Do You Share a Vision?** Ask a friend who works at a different company (any industry) whom you trust to discuss how leaders "share the vision" at his or her company. Ask what is acceptable, what works, and what doesn't work. Relate this to your organization and identify how you can incorporate this information into your efforts to improve how you describe your compelling image of the future.

- **Join Toastmasters:** Join a local Toastmasters group to gain skills that will help you deliver an inspiring vision. Find more information at www.Toastmasters.org.

- **Vision Verification:** Post the current organization vision on a flip-chart page. Gather together your peers and the people who report directly to you. Discuss what a vision is, that it is more than just words on a piece of paper; a vision should paint a picture of a desired future state. Let them know that reaching a shared vision is important. Create a discussion around the following questions:
  - What does this vision statement say to you?
  - How will your job be different once the vision is achieved?
  - What is your role in achieving the vision?
  - What do you need (training, skills, resources) to be better able to help achieve the vision?
  - If you could, how would you improve the principles and beliefs statement? How would this improve the organization? Is this something we should pursue?
  - What will you do differently as a result of this discussion?

12. I appeal to others to share an exciting dream of the future.

Questions You Can Ask

- How do you interpret this item?
- What are your team members' dreams of the future?
- How do you ask others about their future dreams?
- How often do you invite others to share an exciting dream of their future? How much time do you allow for this?
- Why do you think this behavior is important?
- Imagine that you had all the time in the world to listen to others' dreams; how much time do you think it would take to hear everyone in your department's future dreams?
- What could you do to help employees begin to connect their dreams and the organization's vision?
- How do you feel about discussing your team members' desire to share an exciting future?

Activities You Can Suggest

- **Inspiring Leaders:** A huge performance issue organizations face is inspiring leadership at all levels. Kevin Cashman, author of *Leadership from the Inside Out,* studied the most effective clients he had coached over the last thirty years to determine the most effective results-producing leaders. He learned that a leader who inspires others and lives the vision embodies three principles:
  1. *Authenticity:* Self-awareness that openly faces strengths, vulnerabilities, and development challenges.
  2. *Influence:* Communication that connects with people by reminding themselves and others what is genuinely important.
  3. *Value creation:* Passion and aspiration to serve multiple constituencies—self, team, organization, family, community—to sustain performance.

  Review the three principles and explore three essential questions:
     - How can I enhance my authenticity as a leader?
     - How can I extend the influence I have?
     - How can I create more value?

  Use these skills to identify your next strategy to encourage others to share the exciting dream of the future.

- **What's the Plan?** Share your organization's strategic plan with your employees. Review it with them. Answer their questions, which may include:
  - When was the plan developed?
  - Who was involved?
  - What process was used to develop the plan?
  - What data was used to develop the plan?

  Ask them questions as well, such as:
  - What are the key themes of this strategic plan?
  - What are the different messages for each group of people?
  - How is our department (area, group) represented in this plan?
  - How does this strategic plan affect what you do on a daily basis?
  - How does this strategy lead us to our organization's vision?
  - How many of you have a strategic plan for your future?
  - How do your desires for the future fit into this plan?
- **Dream Day:** Invite your team members to bring pictures (a photo, something from a magazine, or one they have drawn) of their future dreams. Ask them to share their "dreams" at the next staff meeting. Post the pictures on a bulletin board or on a wall.

17. I show others how their long-term interests can be realized by enlisting in a common vision.

Questions You Can Ask

- How do you interpret this item?
- What is your greatest challenge with this behavior?
- What excites you about this behavior?
- How satisfied are your team members with the current status of their work?
- What examples can you share when this was an easy, natural fit?
- What examples can you share when you had to work hard to find a way for someone's interest to fit within the vision? How did you feel when it happened?
- Imagine that everyone in your department/organization had an interest that not only fit within the vision, but supported it; what would it be like?
- What are your team members' strengths and opportunities for growth? How does this affect your ability to follow through on this skill?

Activities You Can Suggest

- **Predict the Future:** Alan Kay said, "The best way to predict the future is to invent it." Being prepared is important. Meet with your employees and ask them to invent their future. How would they describe their preferred future? What would they like to be doing? How would they be a part of the organization? You might begin by meeting with them as a group to brainstorm ideas. Follow this up with individual meetings to clarify their goals. When possible, let them know how their interests can be a part of the future of the organization.

- **You Are There:** How will you and others know you have arrived at your ideal and unique image of the future? How will you and they know everyone's interests have been served? Write your answers to these questions. Describe what the future looks like in as concrete a way as you can.

- **Personal Goal:** Meet with your employees to explore their interests. Ask them to identify personal goals that they have and to list them on a piece of paper. Beneath the goals, have them create two columns. Label the first column "Activities" and the second "Performance." In the first column have them list all the steps (activities) they need to take to reach their goals, and in the second column list all the measures that will tell them whether they have been successful with the steps from the first column. For example, if someone's personal goal is to visit Europe with the family five years from now and he or she expect it to require $12,000, some of the activities in the first column might be "save money" and "determine an itinerary." The second column might include "save $200 every month," "buy a travel book to explore possible countries," or "talk to people who have made the trip." The first column is a list of activities that need to be undertaken. The second column—performance—measures whether the activities were actually completed or not. Tell them that you would also like to work with them on their professional interests and that they should begin thinking about their professional goals and how they can be realized.

- **What's Important?** Hold conversations with your direct reports about what's important to each of them. Questions you might use include:
  - What is most important to you in your professional life?
  - Why is that important to you?
  - If you could create the perfect situation, what would it be?
  - How can I support you?

- **Send Stars Away:** No one want to see a star employee leave, someone who has leadership potential in the organization. Stars work hard. They do a great job. You become dependent on them. However, there may come a time when you must move them out of your area. Perhaps they are bored with the jobs they are in. Maybe they are ready for additional responsibilities. You may suspect they are floating their use the inflections. At these times you need to identify available job openings within the organization to prevent them from leaving. Meet with your supervisor when these instances present themselves. Ask for your supervisor's support in finding an opportunity in some other part of the organization for the "stars." This will be a win-win all the way around: your star employee receives a promotion or a chance at learning a new job; you are recognized as someone who cares about the success of your team members; your supervisor gets to help out another area by providing a productive employee; and the organization benefits because it keeps a great employee.
- **If This, Then What?** Make a list of the most important aspirations of your team members. Then, for each aspiration, make a link to how the aspiration can be realized by aligning with the shared vision.
- **Let's Go for Coffee:** Invite two or three of your most promising team members to coffee or a quick lunch. Learn as much as you can so that you can support them. You might consider the following questions:
  - Ask them about their long-term interests and their career aspirations.
  - Ask what learning experiences they believe they need.
  - Ask whether you are providing enough information about advancement opportunities.
  - Ask how they see themselves fitting into the organization's future.
  - Ask whether they have enough time to acquire the knowledge and skills needed.
  - Ask whether they require more advice and guidance and from whom.
  - Ask whether they understand the relationship between their personal development and the goals and strategies of the organization.
  - Ask to what extent they believe that their capabilities are being used.

Take good notes. Compile them. Put a plan of action together for these individuals. More importantly, review what you learned about yourself and how you express the opportunities for success within the organization's vision. Do you believe these employees are representative of all your employees? Do you view your responsibility differently with some employees than others? What do you need to do more often? What do you need to do less? What do you need to start doing to help your employees see how their interests can be realized?

22. I paint the "big picture" of what we aspire to accomplish.

Questions You Can Ask

- What is the "big picture"? What is the larger context in which your vision and the team's vision fit? Think of it as a jigsaw puzzle and you and each team member have a piece of the puzzle. What is the picture on the cover of the puzzle box?
- Tell me how you do this—paint the "big picture"?
- Imagine that you are an artist, and describe the picture. What colors are you using? What size is the picture? What's the frame look like? What is in the background? What is the biggest object? What's the weather like? Are there any people in the picture? What are they doing?
- What year do you anticipate accomplishing your vision? Where will you be? What about your employees?
- Why do you think it is important to paint a picture?
- Imagine that you really could paint a "big picture" of the future. How could you do it?
- What's the most important aspect of this behavior?
- How do you rate your enthusiasm about the future?

Activities You Can Suggest

- **Set Clear Expectations:** Paint the big picture, and take it down to the individual level so your employees can see how they help accomplish the organizational aspirations. Make a list of performance and behavioral expectations for your employees overall, and specifically for individuals as their jobs require. The list should include such things as the way they should deal with you, customers, others in and out of the organization, and each other on work-related matters. Update your list regularly as new issues emerge or the work environment changes. Personally meet with the entire staff to go over the list. Meet with individuals quarterly to review the unique expectations applicable to them. Ensure that they see how they fit into the big picture.

- **Deal Directly:** Fight the urge to avoid those employees who are difficult to deal with, annoying, marginally productive, or who possess similarly unpleasant attributes. Supervisory-employee alienation is a prime factor in a deteriorating relationship and reduces greatly a supervisor's willingness to address issues. Avoiding some employees is noted by all employees and can reduce the enthusiasm and inspiration of all employees. Know what all staff members are working on. Keep up with their progress. Listen to their concerns. This inspires everyone. Give yourself a monthly grade about how well you are doing to ensure that everyone understands his or her role in reaching the group's aspirations.

- **Visualize the Destination:** In *The Leadership Challenge,* we talk about leadership being a journey and that you need to begin the journey with the destination in mind. As a leader, you need to set long-term goals based on your principles and vision for the future. Have you documented your principles and long-term goals based on your vision of the future? Visualization is an important tool to develop this. If you do not have a personal vision statement, begin to establish a one. Write your vision statement; share it with your supervisor, mentor, or coach, and obtain feedback. Take this to the next step and ask your employees to write their personal vision statements. Meet with them individually and help them tie their interests to the organization's vision.

- **Create a Story:** Create the story of your organization in the future. You might start the story with, "Imagine this department in 2020 when. . . ." Use your employees in the starring roles; include a story line of 110 percent success at meeting goals; and add a few futuristic events, like: We no longer need email because we are reading each others' needs by telepathy," just to have some fun with it. Share the story and ask employees how they see themselves helping to achieve this future.

- **Paint the Picture—Literally:** Ask someone in your department or bring in someone from the graphic arts department who can do some amateur sketching at your next staff meeting. Meet with them before the staff meeting to explain what you want to do. At the staff meeting, as you are "painting" the picture of the future, have the artist stand at a flip chart and literally "paint" the picture of what you are saying using colored markers. Ask your employees how they see themselves in the picture and have the artist add them to the chart. Hang the picture of the future in some prominent place.

27. I speak with genuine conviction about the higher meaning and purpose of our work.

Questions You Can Ask

- What do you think genuine conviction means and how do you demonstrate it?
- What is the higher meaning and purpose of the kind of work you do?
- What causes people to become passionate about their work?
- Why is this important to the ability to Inspire a Shared Vision?
- How would others describe your presentation skills?
- What's possible for you to do that would excite others?
- What is the passion that you bring to this work? How do you demonstrate it?
- If Hollywood made a movie of your life, what convictions and passions would they use to create your character?
- Imagine that you accomplished your vision in record time—you reached it. How will the organization be better? How will the industry be better? How will mankind be better?

Activities You Can Suggest

- **Understanding the Organization's Vision:** Work with someone you rarely get to work with, but with whom you would like to build a working relationship because you admire the way he or she thinks and works within the vision of the organization. Your goal is to explore what you each need to do to better understand the vision so that you can speak with conviction about the higher meaning and purpose of your work. Use these questions as a starting point for your exploration:
  - Who are the people who are important for us to learn from?
  - What or who influences the organization's vision?
  - How are decisions made with regard to the vision? Do we know of challenging situations?
  - What are the key goals for the organization? For our departments? For us? Do we see a clear line of delineation from one to another and back to the vision?
  - What are the best communication methods in the organization? Is that the best way to communicate the vision? How could we improve our means of communicating the vision?
  - Do we know when we should speak up about something and when it is best to be silent?

- Do we know exactly when and how we should hold others accountable for living the vision?
- How would we rate ourselves for speaking with conviction about the work we do?
- Do any of our responses bother us enough to discuss them with our supervisors or our coaches?

- **The Famous:** Sometimes is it *how* you say it. Who comes to mind who speaks (or spoke) to others with confidence, conviction, and authenticity? People like Gandhi, Lou Holtz, Jack Canfield, Tom Crum, the Dalai Lama, Catherine McCarthy, Suze Orman, Martin Luther King, Jr., Bill Gates, Steve Jobs, Zig Zigler? Identify other individuals who speak persuasively. What common denominator do you observe in all of them? If possible find video clips of some of their speeches. (In the future, if you are trying to explain this skill to some of your team members, play the speeches for them and ask them to identify what they see.) How can what you learned propel you forward? What will you do differently when speaking about the work you do?

- **Coaching for Confidence and Conviction:** Divide a page of paper in half with a line from top to bottom. On the left write down all the things that you do that you believe display confidence and conviction when discussing the meaning and purpose of your work. On the right, list all the things that you do that get in the way of displaying confidence and conviction about your work. Meet with your supervisor or coach. Ask him or her to appraise your perceptions. Ask for advice about how to move more things out of the right-hand column and how to move more things into the left column. Ask for other suggestions about what you need to do. Schedule a follow-up meeting two weeks out. In the meantime, try some of the suggestions and be prepared to report on them at your next meeting.

- **Who's the Most Passionate of Them All?** Identify two individuals in your organization you believe have the most passion about the work you do. Ask whether you can get on their calendars. If they are outside driving range, a phone call will do; however, a personal visit is much better. Ask them whether they like what they do and why. Ask what it is about the job that makes them as dedicated as they are. Ask them about the future of the organization. Ask them about the most important aspects of their jobs. Your goal is not to quiz them about this skill, but instead to identify what they say and do that displays their confidence and conviction.
  - What do you hear? What do you see?
  - How do they speak? What is their tone, inflection?
  - What kinds of words do you use? Jot them down.

- What non-verbals do you observe?
- What do their faces look like?

After your meetings, note your observations and identify things that you can do. Expect to be inspired.

- **Find Passion on the Streets:** Find people who have a passion for what they do. It might be your son's third-grade teacher. It might be the owner of the mom-and-pop pizza shop in your neighborhood. It doesn't matter who it is. Meet the people and talk with them personally. What makes them tick? How does conviction about what they do come through for each person? Make a list. How can you translate this to your work?

- **Orientation Presentation:** Volunteer to write and give a presentation at the next new employee orientation that presents the higher meaning and purpose of the organization's work. Clear it with your supervisor.

- **Tell the World:** Prepare a speech you could give to the Chamber of Commerce, Civic League, or others that explains the organization's vision and the higher meaning and purpose of the organization's work. Have your supervisor or coach critique it.

- **Your Values and the Work You Do:** It is easier to speak with genuine conviction about the higher meaning and purpose of work when you are clear about your values. It is even easier if your personal goals, values, and vision are aligned with the organization's goals, values, and vision. Don't have a personal vision yet? Take the next month to write your personal vision and goals—for you, for your life. You may wish to check this website for help in creating your personal vision statement: http://humanresources.about.com/od/success/a/personal_vision.htm.

  What are your values? Compare your values with the organization's values. Are they congruent? If not, why not? Use this information to clarify your leadership philosophy. Then decide how you will share this information with your team, ensuring that you can speak to the higher meaning and purpose of the work the team does.

BOOKS, ARTICLES, AND WEBSITES

Books for Inspire a Shared Vision

- Warren Bennis, Gretchen M. Spreitzer, and Thomas G. Cummings (Eds.). *The Future of Leadership: Today's Top Leadership Thinkers Speak to Tomorrow's Leaders*. San Francisco: Jossey-Bass, 2001.

- Boyd Clarke and Ron Crossland. *The Leader's Voice: How Your Communication Can Inspire Action and Get Results!* New York: Select Books, 2002.
- Belle Linda Halpren and Kathy Lubar. *Leadership Presence: Dramatic Techniques to Reach Out, Motivate, and Inspire*. New York: Gotham Books, 2003.
- Gary Hamel. *Leading the Revolution*. Boston: Harvard Business School Press, 2002.
- Jennifer James. *Thinking in the Future Tense: Leadership Skills for the New Age*. New York: Simon & Schuster, 1996.
- John Naisbitt. *Mindset: Eleven Ways to Change the Way You See—and Create—the Future*. New York: HarperCollins, 2006.
- Burt Nanus. *Visionary Leadership*. San Francisco: Jossey-Bass, 1992.
- Peter Schwartz. *The Art of the Long View*. New York: Currency, 1996.
- Bruce Sterling. *Tomorrow Now: Envisioning the Next Fifty Years*. New York: Random House, 2003.
- Margaret Wheatley. *Leadership and the New Science*. San Francisco: Berrett-Koehler, 1992.

Articles

- "The HBR List: Breakthrough Ideas for 2008," *Harvard Business Review,* February 2008. HBR's annual snapshot of the emerging shape of business.
- "The Five Competitive Forces That Shape Strategy," *Harvard Business Review,* January 2008. Awareness of the five forces can help a company understand the structure of its industry and stake out a position that is more profitable and less vulnerable to attack.
- "Using the Balanced Scorecard as a Strategic Management System," *Harvard Business Review,* July 2007. In 1992, Robert S. Kaplan and David P. Norton's concept of the balanced scorecard revolutionized conventional thinking about performance metrics. By going beyond traditional measures of financial performance, the concept has given a generation of managers a better understanding of how their companies are really doing.
- *Harvard Business Review*, July/August 2008. Special HBR Centennial Issue about how businesses hone their competitive edge.

Websites/Blogs

- www.businessweek.com. Features and interesting articles about business.
- www.hbr.org. *Harvard Business Review*. A copy of the article titled "The Secrets to Successful Strategy Execution," which represents the idea that

success will only occur if decision-making authority and information flow are identified.

- www.money.cnn.com/magazines/fortune. Special features and recent articles from *Fortune* magazine.
- www.summary.com. Soundview Executive Book Summaries are 5,000-word, eight-page distillations of specially selected business books. Soundview subscribers receive two or three eight-page summaries of the best business books each month (thirty per year).
- www.Toastmasters.org. To locate a local Toastmasters group to practice presentations and for other speaking information.
- www.wsj.com. *Wall Street Journal* contact.
- www.wfs.org. *The Futurist* magazine contact.

HOW THE COACH MODELS THIS PRACTICE

- ◆ Discuss current and future trends of coaching and how you and the leader will interact.
- ◆ Describe the image of success that awaits the leader at the end of the coaching experience.
- ◆ Enlist the leader to share his or her aspirations of leadership, the kind of leader he or she would like to be, and his or her professional goals.
- ◆ Demonstrate how the leader's goal can be a part of your image of having another successful client.
- ◆ Describe the end of the relationship using passionate, exciting words that appeal to the leader's objectives, using metaphors and analogies to paint a vivid picture of the leader's success.
- ◆ Allow your passion for your work as a professional coach to shine through, demonstrating that you expect success.

CHAPTER 4: COACHING TO CHALLENGE THE PROCESS

In This Chapter

- Review the Challenge the Process practice.
- List the corresponding commitments.
- Identify the six LPI items that reference this practice.
- Examine potential questions and activities a coach could use.
- Provide additional resources.
- Consider how the coach could model this practice.

Challenge the Process is the practice that ensures that the organization is on the cutting edge. The leader and the rest of the team are on constant alert to identify areas of process improvement and then take calculated risks to use creative solutions to improve the process. The work of the leader is change, and change is here to stay. It is what makes organizations more competitive. Change can bring out the best in people because they are pushed to dig deep into their reserves and to tap into uncharted talent. Change forces people to be innovative, to experiment with new processes, and to find ways to be more effective and efficient. Change can also create havoc and produce resistance when leadership skills are not evident. To effectively challenge the process, leaders must Search for Opportunities and Experiment and Take Risks.

SEARCH FOR OPPORTUNITIES

Opportunities for improvement exist everywhere. Sometimes they fall in a leader's lap; at other times leaders need to search them out. Sometimes leaders have to shake things up; at other times they just need to grab onto the adversity that surrounds them. Whether change comes from outside threats or internal challenges, each presents the leader with an opportunity. Leaders make things happen by seizing these opportunities and relying on outsight to actively seek innovative ideas from outside the boundaries of familiar experience.

Leaders make change happen, which requires that leaders actively seek ways to make things better, to grow, innovate, and improve. To Search for Opportunities to get extraordinary things done, leaders make use of two essentials:

- Seize the initiative
- Exercise outsight

Seize the initiative. Leaders are people who seize opportunities for improvement with enthusiasm, determination, and a desire to make something happen. They embrace the challenge presented by the shifts in their industries or the new demands of the marketplace and commit themselves to creating exciting new possibilities that make a meaningful difference. Change requires leadership; it requires someone to step up to the plate and find the way through. Leaders need to be innovative. Leaders also need to support initiative in others, encouraging them to speak up, to offer suggestions for improvement, and to be straightforward about their constructive criticism. Leaders challenge the status quo to make things better. Leaders challenge others to help them stretch, grow, and develop their skills. Leaders pair this challenge with encouragement, tapping into people's hearts and minds.

Exercise outsight. As leaders seize initiatives for change, they must also be cognizant of external realities. They must be outwardly focused on staying in touch with customers, employees, stockholders, students, suppliers, vendors, business partners, managers, and others the world over. Improving processes requires more communication than does routine work. Demand for change will come from inside as well as outside the organization. In the same way, ideas to make improvements must come from inside as well as outside the organization. Exemplary leaders promote external and internal communication, they let ideas flow freely from the outside into the organization, and, probably most important, leaders prepare themselves to welcome the next challenge that comes their way. Leaders welcome new challenges when they know what inspires them to do their best every day.

EXPERIMENT AND TAKE RISKS

To pursue passions and fulfill their dreams, leaders must do the unorthodox. This means taking risks with bold ideas. It is clear why this is true: Nothing new and great is achieved by doing things the way they've always been done. Leaders test unproven strategies and break out of the norms that box the average person in. They get extraordinary things done in organizations because they are willing to Experiment and Take Risks.

Leaders can transform challenge into an exploration, uncertainty into a sense of adventure, fear into resolve, and risk into reward. This happens when leaders create a climate in which the norm is to Experiment and Take Risks. To make this happen it is essential for leaders to:

- Generate small wins
- Learn from experience

Generate small wins. One of the biggest challenges for leaders trying to improve processes is to get people to want to move in a new direction, to break old mind-sets, and to change existing behavior patterns. These are all important in order to tackle big problems and attempt extraordinary performance. Exemplary leaders do this step-by-step through the generation of small wins. The most effective change processes are incremental, not one giant leap. Each step creates a "win" that propels people to continue in that direction. Wins generate excitement, energy, and commitment. This means that leaders must break down big problems into small, doable actions and that they may need to try a lot of little things when initiating something new before they get it right. Leaders may call these small steps pilot studies, demonstration projects, lab tests, field experiments, trial runs, or market trials. What leaders call them is not critical; however, it is critical that they try lots of little things that can potentially create something much bigger. These small wins produce results because they form the basis for a consistent pattern of winning that attracts people who want to be allied with a successful venture. Small wins build people's confidence and reinforce their natural desire to feel successful. Small wins produce results because they build personal and group commitment to a course of action.

Learn from experience. None of us do a thing perfectly the first time we try it. Learning through trial and error is an important part of the learning process. This requires learning by doing. This is true for everything we do, whether we are learning to snowboard, play bridge, or bake a soufflé. It is also true for making improvements on the job and even learning to be a leader. How can leaders do this? The first thing is to create a climate for learning, an environment in which mistakes become a learning experience for everyone. The safer people feel, the more risks they will take and the more mistakes they will be willing to make. A learning environment requires leaders to maintain a positive attitude about learning. Exemplary leaders are active learners, approaching each new and unfamiliar experience with a willingness to learn, an appreciation for the importance of learning, and a recognition that learning involves making some mistakes. Leaders who view change as a challenge and an opportunity to learn transform stressful events into manageable situations. Leaders assist their constituents to cope more effectively by creating a climate that develops hardiness by building a sense of control, that offers more rewards than punishment, and that encourages people to see change as full of possibilities.

Challenge the Process is a critical leadership skill in this time of change. It requires that leaders be adept at identifying process improvements and encouraging others to be willing to engage in the practice of searching for and remedying processes in order to save time, money, and resources, as well as please customers. Further, it means that leaders and their teams consistently search for faster, better, cheaper wins for the organization. In summary, Challenge the Process is girded by two commitments.

- **Commitment 5:** Search for opportunities by seizing the initiative and by looking outward for innovative ways to improve.
- **Commitment 6:** Experiment and take risks by consistently generating small wins and learning from experience.

Challenge the Process is a time for leaders to recognize the importance of going against the grain to do what is right—and to remember that they are not in it alone. Leaders can ask others to assist, get some coaching, find a friend to lean on, and remember that others need the same kind of encouragement.

CHALLENGE THE PROCESS: PRACTICE FOR THE LPI ITEMS

The following six statements refer to the items in the *LPI: Leadership Practices Inventory* that relate to Challenge the Process. The numbers reference the item number in the LPI. These items are numbered and listed in the order as they appear in the LPI. This is done to make it easy to locate each item in this book; the order in which the items are discussed in this book does not suggest an order of importance. You need to determine, based on your client's feedback, which items your client wants to work on and in what sequence.

After each item, you will find suggested questions and activities. These are created for a coaching situation and may be used with the leader(s) you may be coaching. Several of the activities reference a "journal." There is an assumption that your leader will have a personal journal in which to track plans, questions, and desires. A journal is an important tool for reflection on a leader's journey to excellence.

Note: There are many more activities than you would ever use with one person. Work with your client to identify one that will be most useful. Even better, have your clients create their own after you present some possibilities. Remember, the value of these activities and discussion questions is not in the doing, but in the follow-on discussion with you, the coach. Be sure to allow time to discuss the "so what" and the "now what" that occur as a result of any discussion or activity.

At the end of this chapter you will find a resource list that includes books, articles, websites, and blogs for you or your client to use. You will also find a section titled "How the Coach Models This Practice," which serves as a reminder to you about what you must do to be a positive, proactive model for your client.

3. I seek out challenging opportunities that test my own skills and abilities.

Questions You Can Ask

- How do you interpret this item?
- What's the greatest risk you've taken and how did it feel?
- What part of the status quo do you think needs challenging? What would happen if you did that?
- Why do you think you rated the way that you did on this behavior?
- What can be fun about seeking challenging opportunities?
- If you placed all the organization's leaders on a continuum that measured willingness to seek challenging opportunities, where would you place yourself?
- Why is this an important aspect of leadership?

- Where would you turn to gain support for improving this area of leadership?
- What needs to be fixed in this organization?

Activities You Can Suggest

- **New Hobby:** Take up a new hobby or sport. Observe the support systems you require that allow you to adjust to this hobby, for example, how do you find time, who helps you with other responsibilities, what lifestyle changes have you made? Support system changes are required for successful changes to occur—even with the start of a hobby. Think about how this relates to the support systems required to allow change to occur efficiently at your organization.
- **Job Rotation:** Work with your supervisor to identify a job in another part of the organization that would allow you to learn new skills. Make arrangements to rotate into the job for an agreed-on amount of time. Use this opportunity to practice some of the skills that you need to improve based on what you and your supervisor have identified. Foreign assignments, new projects, startups, working in a virtual environment, and other such opportunities create unique challenges that stretch and grow leaders. These are opportunities to push yourself to obtain some of those other skills and to take you out of your comfort zone.
- **Performance:** Examine your own performance on the job. Identify the two or three things that you know you need to improve. Write them down, create a plan for improvement, and get to work. During your next performance review with your supervisor, compile your notes and be prepared to participate in the discussion to learn whether you are heading on the right track. If your review is some time away, don't hesitate to meet with your supervisor earlier to obtain more feedback and ideas.
- **Development Plan Input:** The purpose of this activity is to gain insight into your development plan from leaders in other areas in the organization. This is helpful in two different ways. First, it doubles or triples the number of ideas and feedback you obtain. Second, and more important, you have a chance to see your development from another part of the organization. This cross-functional perspective is often a missing experience for new leaders. To complete this activity, identify one or two individuals who are not in your line of supervision with whom to share your development plans. Schedule a

meeting with them. Prepare your questions ahead of time. Questions should include things such as:

- I would like to _____. Is that reasonable?
- What are your thoughts about my long- and short-term goals?
- If I were in your department (area), what would you suggest for me?
- What learning experiences do you suggest I complete to achieve my short- and long-term goals?
- How does my plan link to your department and its strategies and goals?
- What learning opportunities can you suggest that will round out my competencies as a future leader?
- What should I have asked you about?

After each interview, return to your supervisor or coach and share what you learned.

- **Volunteer to Conduct a Special Assignment:** Tell your supervisor that you would like to conduct a special assignment for which he or she feels you are qualified, for example, something that requires coordination among several departments. State that you hope that the assignment is also a stretch for you. During the assignment, keep a list of all the skills required for the assignment. Rate yourself on each of the skills. Be candid and provide why you rated yourself as you did: What did you do well? What do you need to improve? Midway through the project, and again at the end of the project, review what happened with your supervisor. Ask your supervisor to provide feedback to you about your skills. How does your supervisor's assessment compare to yours? For those skills for which there is a gap between your assessment and your supervisor's assessment, try to reconcile the differences. For those for which you both agree improvement is required, identify learning experiences in which you can participate to gain new skills and knowledge.

- **Chair a Committee:** Volunteer to chair a committee for your department. Ask your supervisor to consider you for any upcoming opportunities. You will learn a great deal. If you have never chaired a committee, you will be amazed at how much knowledge and the number of skills that are required. This learning opportunity will most likely result in a list of other skills you may wish to sharpen. Maintain a list of these skills and discuss with your supervisor other opportunities for growth when your committee has completed its work.

- **Friendly Growth Opportunities:** Invite several friends over for a backyard cookout or a potluck dinner. Let them know that you have an ulterior motive. You want them each to discuss the events that they have participated in that led to the most personal and professional growth for them. Use these ideas as a springboard for identifying the kinds of ideas that will be most helpful to you.
- **Read:** Make it a practice to read one book each month that will help you develop as a leader. These can be biographies and/or books about management, leadership, strategy, communication, skill development, or other related topics.
- **Lectures:** Scan the newspaper for lecture series sponsored by a community college or a civic group. Keep an eye out for other learning opportunities in your community.
- **Develop the Strategy:** Tell your supervisor that you would like to participate on the team that develops the next strategic plan for the organization.
- **Select a Challenge:** Identify a challenge that you've always wanted to do, for example, run a half-marathon, learn to tango, or learn gourmet cooking. Plot a timeline to accomplish your challenge. During your challenge, track your thoughts and feelings along the way. Determine what works for you and what doesn't. How are you motivated? What gets in the way of your progress? How do you manage your time? Is it better to do this with a partner or alone? At the end of the timeline, did you meet your challenge? What did you learn about yourself? What did you learn about your performance? What does this tell you about how you learn? About your ability to assess yourself? How can you put what you learned into practice at work?
- **Attend a Self-Awareness Seminar:** Often held with small groups, a self-awareness seminar will help you assess your developmental needs beyond skills and knowledge. They get to the deeper meaning of who you are and why you do what you do. You could begin with www.NTL.org or www.LandmarkEducation.com.

8. I challenge people to try out new and innovative ways to do their work.

Questions You Can Ask

- How do you interpret this item?
- How do your employees know it is all right for them to use innovative ways to complete their work?

- What messages do you send your employees in the form of statements and questions that you approve of this behavior? How often?
- How well prepared are your team members to identify and select ways to improve their work processes?
- What's the last thing your group did that was innovative?
- How could your innovations have an effect on the company?
- Can you share a couple of examples of how you celebrated the last few innovations?
- Can you give me a couple of examples of mistakes that your employees made and what happened?
- How do you make it safe for people to try different ways to do their work?

Activities You Can Suggest

- **Problem-Solving Tools:** It is easier to tackle problems with tools available. Before you challenge your employees to try new approaches, suggest that they go to www.mindtools.com/pages/main/newMN_TMC.htm to learn more about problem-solving techniques. They will learn which tool to select for various kinds of situations.
- **Pros and Cons:** Identify a situation and enlist your employees to identify new approaches. Teach them to use a pro and con listing to identify the best of possible new approaches. Ask them to return to you with a possible solution.
- **Don't Do It Alone:** Lots of people try to solve all the problems by themselves. This is not a good idea. If you are one of those people, try this idea next time. Even if you know you have an answer, find an employee who can act as a sounding board for you. Tell him or her about the problem. Your goal should not just be to find a solution, but to try to gain clearer focus on the problem itself. Bounce your solution off the other person. Discuss the vision and how the solution relates to the vision. Ask whether there is a better solution—one that is tied more closely to the vision. Get in the habit of asking for help when solving problems. It is good coaching for your employees.
- **First Things First:** Correctly defining a problem and identifying its root cause are the first and most important steps. They ensure that you are working on a cause— not a symptom. Ensure that your employees know how to identify a root cause.
- **Strategy Shuffle:** Want to give employees a chance to share ideas for solving problems? Try this all-employee problem-solving tool. Hold a meeting with your

team members. Ask them all to write brief descriptions of a problem or situation for which they want ideas, for example, "Addressing an angry customer." Next they are to list what they have tried. They should not write their names on the papers. Collect the pages and shuffle them a bit. Pass them around the group so that everyone receives someone else's. Tell them that they should quickly read the problem and what has been tried and add ideas at the bottom. Once they have added their ideas, they pass them to the left and receive the page from the right. Again, read what has been written and add another idea. Continue to pass the sheets of paper around the table, with each person offering his or her most creative strategies for addressing the problem, until the pages are filled. When they have their own papers back, they can read what has been written and add new ideas. In the end, collect all the papers and hang them on a wall so that all employees can read their own solutions as well as those of others.

- **Build a Playground:** Find a community project for which your team could volunteer to complete something in a couple of mornings. It could be to build a playground, make small repairs on homes for the elderly, or complete a "clean-up" project. Spend time at the end of each event to review "what we did well" and "what we would like to do better" as a team. "What approaches could we implement at work?" Activities like these not only build skills, but they are also good team-building events, and helping the community is good PR for your organization.

- **Review an Event:** Set time aside with your team members following their next project to analyze how they did. How did they work as a team? What worked? What didn't work? What can be improved before the next project? How can you help them?

- **Four Questions:** Before you challenge people to try a new approach, remember that every employee wants four questions answered during times of change:
  - What is happening?
  - Why is it happening?
  - How will this affect me and my job?
  - What's the plan for getting there?

The next time a change is about to occur, take time to discuss these questions with your employees. If you want your employees to try new approaches in general, be prepared to have a discussion around these same questions to introduce the concept.

- **Send a Note:** Recognition for a job well done is a top motivator for employee performance. Team members are motivated by personal, thoughtful recognition. Send a personal, handwritten note to an employee who has suggested a process improvement or a creative idea—even if it cannot be used at this time. (Yes, you can email or text message; it depends on how impressive and memorable you would like the recognition to be.)
- **Beyond the Competition:** Identify local competitors. List all the reasons customers may find them more attractive than your organization. With your team, brainstorm a list for each reason of at least five ways the organization could move beyond the competition. Invite employees to try out some of the ideas.
- **Bugs Me List:** Brainstorm a list with your team members about everything that "bugs" them on the job. Identify possible ways to reduce this list.

13. I actively search for innovative ways to improve what we do.

Questions You Can Ask

- How would you define "actively search"? Where do you search? In different countries? On the Internet? To your competition?
- How much time do you spend searching for innovative ideas?
- Where do you go to find new ideas?
- Where do you feel most creative?
- What would happen if you had all the time in the world to search for innovative ideas?
- How can you help your employees search beyond themselves for answers?
- Imagine that you have been assigned to be the Innovation Czar at your company. What are the first things you would do?
- How difficult is this to complete? What would have to occur to make it easier?

Activities You Can Suggest

- **Call a Customer, or Two:** Create a list of customers—internal or external. Invite them to lunch (or make a phone call) and ask them what things they would like your department to do differently than you are now.

- **Change Website:** Searching for innovative ideas hints that change is in the air. Understanding various steps to making change is important. Check out the website created by Rick Maurer, author of *Beyond the Wall of Resistance,* at www .rickmaurer.com. It is jam packed with more than one hundred articles, tips, and tools in change categories such as Getting Started, Leading Change, Keeping Change Alive, Getting Back on Track, and Making a Compelling Case for Change. Many of these will lead you to ideas for innovative improvements.

- **Interview a Leader:** Interview individuals in your community or neighborhood who are leaders in another industry. Ask them what they do to prepare for innovation; how they establish support systems; where they look for ideas; and what they think is the most important. Bring the information back and share it with your co-workers. How can what you learned be implemented in your organization?

- **Visit the Competition:** Identify several competitors. Divide your team into sub-teams and assign each team a competitor. Have them visit the competitors with an open mind. What are they doing better? What could we learn from them? What do we do better, and how could we make it even better? If your competition does not have a place of business your team members could visit, have them compare websites.

- **Keep the Competitive Edge:** Create a matrix. Across the top list all the aspects that your organization wants to do better than all the rest, for example, reduce turnover, decrease time, increase sales, increase repeat customers. Include a grade (A to F) for how well you think you are doing. In the vertical column on the left list the organizations you see as your competition in the area. Go across and realistically compare them to each of the aspects in the row at the top. How is your organization doing? What can you do better? Are any of your competitors closing in on those aspects that set you apart? What creative things can you do that will continue to give the organization the competitive edge?

- **Volunteer for Innovation:** Lead a volunteer team from work to participate in different events. Here are several suggestions:
  - One-time community service team, such as a spring neighborhood cleanup day or serving in a soup kitchen.
  - Emergency disaster relief, such as holding a yard sale to raise money for families who were in a local fire or flood.

- Support a local event, such as building a float for the local Thanksgiving Day parade or sponsoring a fun run team or parking cars.
- Support other volunteer efforts, such as youth going to another state or country to provide aid or assistance.

After the event, review what happened. How was the event handled differently by the organizing group? What could you transfer to your department?

- **Elevator Speech:** Create an elevator speech, a short, three-sentence speech that defines why innovative and creative thinking are important to the organization or to your department. Share this with your employees and enlist their help to search for innovative ways outside your organization.
- **Join a Local Volunteer Group:** Join your local Civic League, Rotary, Kiwanis, or other volunteer organization. Observe how the group manages its business. Often there is something for you to learn from groups that run on a shoestring budget. Can you implement anything in your department?
- **How Do You Monitor?** Ask a friend who works at a different company (any industry) to discuss the monitoring process used at his or her company. Ask how people ensure that they are measuring the right things, what works, and what doesn't work. Take this activity one step further if you can, and relate it to the discussions you have at your staff meetings to identify how you can incorporate this information into your efforts to improve.
- **Take a Field Trip:** Take your team on a field trip to stimulate creativity. Where? Here are a few possibilities: a toy store, a discount store, the zoo, a museum, or a factory tour (preferably one that hands out free samples at the end). When you return, ask your team: How was what you saw like our business? How was it different? What do they do that we could incorporate here?
- **Subscribe and Read:** Subscribe to and read your industry's journals. What are others in the industry doing that you could build on?
- **See It as a Customer:** Ask co-workers to view the organization from their customers' perspectives. What would the customers want them to do differently or better? Capture these ideas for current or future use. You may wish to create a list (for example, speed, friendliness, accuracy) and track the improvement over several months. To make this come alive, ask your employees to "be" customers by either shopping for the product your organization makes, calling your organization's customer service with a

question, or visiting a store. Ask them to share what happened, and what the organization could do better.

18. I ask "What can we learn?" when things do not go as expected.

Questions You Can Ask

- What's your first reaction when things go wrong? How do you respond? What's your second reaction?
- It is all well and good to say that you look for what you can learn when things go wrong, but what really happens?
- How does the team deal with problems, bad news, or poor decisions?
- How do you think your team feels when things do not go as expected? Why?
- How do you track lessons learned from these experiences?
- What's exciting about mistakes?
- Complete this statement, "Errors are like _____, because _____."
- What would happen if your organization rewarded employees when things went wrong?
- How do you relate to the statement, "If you are not failing, you are not learning"?

Activities You Can Suggest

- **When It Doesn't Go Well:** The next time something does not go as planned, learn from your people. Ask your direct reports to complete the three questions below and provide feedback to you (either written or verbally). Be gracious and accepting with the feedback. In fact, you might consider rewarding anyone who gives you feedback. Once you obtain all the feedback, assess what you need to do. What behaviors should be changed?

    Provide this direction to your team members: "As you review the project, and think about similar future projects, consider what I could have done differently:

    - What would you like me to do more of?
    - What would you like me to do less of?
    - What would you like me to continue the same?"

- **Did You Hear the One About:** The next time something does not go as expected, start your next team meeting with a story overheard in passing, for example, one caterpillar saying to another as a butterfly flew overhead, "You'll never get me up in one of those things!" Ask the group: "What's to be learned here?" Accept all answers. If they have not addressed expectations, ask, "What does the caterpillar's comment tell us about outcomes?" Discuss something along the lines of: "Learn all you need to know about adapting to change, because you can never predict results or when you will be the one 'up in one of those things!' We need to be careful that we do not self-limit ourselves and our possibilities. Like the caterpillar, we have many successes to come."

- **Interview an Exec:** When monitoring and evaluating results, it is important to hear the message from the top of the organization. Generally, senior leaders have a broader perspective. Work with your supervisor to have access to one of the executive/senior leaders. Arrange a discussion with him or her. Here are some questions you might ask the individual:
  - What factors do you think contributed to the results?
  - What could we have done differently?
    - What challenges should we be aware of that our organization will face in the future?
  - What business strategies will require support from us?
  - What competencies will be required to support the business strategies?
  - What advice do you have for us in the future?

  Share what you learn with your team.

- **Learn About Problem Solving:** Managers solve problems. It is that simple. That is a manager's job. Leaders continue to solve problems and they also strategize ahead of the problems to prevent them from occurring. Therefore, it is important to be skilled and knowledgeable about the entire problem-solving process. There are several steps between understanding the root cause and generating a solution. Consider having your team take a class on problem solving. Perhaps you could bring it on-site. You can probably find an online class, and your local community college will definitely offer one. Check with your training department.

- **Process Improvement Team:** Become a member (or leader) of a Lean, Six Sigma, or process improvement team for a community organization for which you volunteer.

- **Customer Service Survey:** Share a copy of your organization's most recent customer service survey with your team members. Discuss possible improvements.

71

23. I identify measurable milestones that keep projects moving forward.

Questions You Can Ask

- How do you interpret this item?
- This behavior is the work of project management. Who is the best project manager on your team?
- Why is it important to establish milestones? Who does the work on these?
- To what extent have your employees challenged your milestones?
- How do you inform your team and track milestones for each project?
- What if you did not establish milestones? Has that ever happened?
- How is a potential process improvement project initiated in your department/ organization?
- What small wins have occurred recently?
- How do you encourage your people to identify achievable small wins?
- Imagine that setting goals and establishing measurable milestones was the most exciting and fun part of your job. What would have to happen to make that true?

Activities You Can Suggest

- **Make Mine a Small Win:** Ask everyone on the team to talk to one of his or her customers, asking one question, "What's one thing I could do that would make your life easier?" Meet with your team and ask them about their results. Post the ideas. Divide your team into pairs or trios. Ask each small group to identify one of the posted items that they would like to address. Allow time for the small groups to establish plans that include measurable timelines and to report back. Depending on the timelines, schedule a meeting for reports back to the group.
- **Establishing Metrics to Monitor:** Projects with metrics have better results. Read Chapter 8, Task VIII: Establishing Metrics, in Jeff Evans and Chuck Schaeffer's *Ten Tasks of Change: Demystifying Changing Organizations*. What insights did you gain?
- **Who Moved My Cheese?** Purchase several copies of Spencer Johnson's *Who Moved My Cheese?* After reading it, pass it throughout the organization. Have everyone take it home to read and sign his or her name in the book after reading

it. After everyone has completed the book, use it to start a discussion about the change an upcoming project may create. You may use some of these questions:

- What was the most important thing you learned about planning and change?
- How does the book's message relate to our department/organization?
- Do we have adequate plans and goals for our upcoming project?
- How could we better plan for the project and its changes?
- How could we better implement the change?
- What does it take to recognize a depleting cheese stock?
- What will you do differently as a result of this discussion?

Other book choices are *Our Iceberg Is Melting* (John Kotter) or *Lessons from the Hive* (Charles Decker).

- **Book a Visit:** Visit a large local bookstore, such as Barnes and Noble. Go to the business book section and pull five books off the shelf that address planning and goal setting. Get a cup of coffee. Page through the books and jot down ten new things you learned that can help you. Be prepared to share these ideas with your team.

28. I take initiative in anticipating and responding to change.

Questions You Can Ask

- Tell me about the kinds of things you have done with your initiative.
- Tell me about the things you would like to initiate.
- How do you relate creativity and initiative?
- How do you anticipate change?
- How do you respond to change? How can you "practice" anticipating and responding to change? Can you practice outside the workplace?
- What types of things change in your business that you should anticipate? What obstacles prevent you from responding to change?
- How could you be the next hero of your company?
- What would you most like to challenge about the organization's status quo? What would happen if you did?
- What two opportunities exist that you could leverage to achieve your objectives in the upcoming year?
- How do you model initiative for your team?

Activities You Can Suggest

- **Challenge Thinking:** Challenge how you think to truly find ways to improve. Here are some suggestions to prompt your own monitoring of strategic leadership issues. Ask yourself these questions:
  - What would we do differently if we really listened to our customers?
  - How can we think about what quality means in our organization?
  - If there were no constraints, what could we be the best in the world at doing? How would that change our organization? Our strategy?
  - What processes and activities are we holding onto that may have outlived their value in today's world?
  - We think of ourselves as an organization that _____; what if we instead thought of ourselves as an organization that _____?
  - What if we openly discussed our undiscussables?

  Review your thoughts with your supervisor or your coach.

- **Teachability Barriers:** Try this personal risk to learn more about yourself. Work with a co-worker to decide whether you have any barriers that get in the way of accurately assessing your behaviors and performance. Barriers might include:
  - *Pride:* You can't be proud and teachable at the same time.
  - *Success:* Your quick climb to the position you now hold could prevent you from seeing that you still have a lot to learn.
  - *Lack of time:* You need to invest time in learning; if you won't invest in you, who will?

  Discuss these and others and determine whether you can assess your own behaviors and performance accurately. If not, where do you need to improve?

- **Substitute for Someone:** If someone is away for a period of time for a vacation or work-related travel, volunteer to substitute for the individual while he or she is out. Ask for and be prepared for lots of feedback, improvement suggestions, and corrective recommendations. It isn't easy to be thrown into a situation like this, but you will learn a great deal about yourself, your skills, and what it takes to do other jobs. Ensure that your supervisor is involved, not just to give you permission to take on the responsibility, but to provide additional feedback and to be ready to coach you through some of the difficult spots.

- **Take Two:** Every leader remembers a time when he or she wishes he or she had done something differently. Ask your supervisor to discuss such a time with you.

Then use the following questions to discuss a time when your supervisor learned a valuable lesson from a difficult situation.

- Tell me about the situation and why you were disappointed in the results.
- What negative impact did it have?
- How risky was this situation?
- What would you have done differently if you had a "Take 2"?
- Was there anything you could do to mitigate what happened?
- What did you do differently after that situation to prevent situations like that from happening again?
- How do you remember to do things differently?
- What advice do you have for me about experimenting and taking risks?

- **Status Quo Challenge:** Ask a friend who works at a different company (any industry) whom you trust to share how employees challenge the status quo at his or her company. Ask what is acceptable, what works, and what doesn't work. Relate this to your organization and identify how you can incorporate this information into your efforts to improve.

- **Entertain a Risk:** Identify a recreational risk such as whitewater rafting, bungee jumping, riding the highest roller coaster, or diving off a high dive. List why it seems risky to you. List why it seems safe to you. If you really want to challenge yourself, actually complete the risky activity. Analyze it afterward: How did you feel before? After? How is this similar to taking a risk at work?

- **Community Work:** It is not uncommon for volunteer and/or community organizations to be filled with redundancy and inefficiencies. Look around at the community organization you support. What could be completed more efficiently? Establish a plan to challenge the status quo by making a suggestion for improvement. Think about:
  - When is the best time to address the issue?
  - To whom will you address the issue?
  - What will you say, for example, what is the reason for a change, what will be better, why is it important?
  - How will you suggest making the change?
  - How will you support the change?

Implement your plan. Share what occurred with your supervisor or your coach if you desire additional feedback.

BOOKS, ARTICLES, AND WEBSITES TO RECOMMEND

Books for Challenge the Process

- Daniel Ariely. *Predictably Irrational: The Hidden Forces That Shape Our Decisions* (rev. ed.). New York: HarperCollins, 2009.
- Elaine Biech. *Thriving Through Change: A Leader's Practical Guide to Change Mastery*. Alexandria, VA: ASTD Press, 2007.
- Arlene Blum. *Annapurna: A Woman's Place* (20th ann. ed.). San Francisco: Sierra Club Books, 1998.
- Mihaly Csikszentmihalyi. *Finding Flow: The Psychology of Engagement with Everyday Life*. New York: Basic Books, 1997.
- Richard Farson and Ralph Keyes. *Whoever Makes the Most Mistakes Wins: The Paradox of Innovation*. New York: The Free Press, 2002.
- Richard Foster and Sarah Kaplan. *Creative Destruction: Why Companies That Are Built to Last Underperform the Market—and How to Successfully Transform Them*. New York: Currency, 2001.
- Bill George. *Seven Lessons for Leading in Crisis*. San Francisco: Jossey-Bass, 2009.
- Malcolm Gladwell. *Blink: The Power of Thinking Without Thinking*. New York: Little, Brown, 2005.
- Gary Hamel with Bill Breen. *The Future of Management*. Boston: Harvard Business School Press, 2007.
- Ronald Heifitz and Marty Linsky. *Leadership on the Line: Staying Alive Through the Dangers of Leading*. Boston: Harvard Business School Press, 2002.
- Rosabeth Moss Kanter, Barry A. Stein, and T.D. Jick. *The Challenge of Organizational Change: How Companies Experience It and Leaders Guide It*. New York: The Free Press, 1992.
- Tom Kelley with Jonathon Littman. *The Art of Innovation: Lessons in Creativity from IDEO, America's Leading Design Firm*. New York: Currency Doubleday, 2005.
- Tom Kelley with Jonathon Littman. *The Ten Faces of Innovation: IDEO's Strategies for Beating the Devil's Advocate & Driving Creativity Throughout Your Organization*. New York: Currency Doubleday, 2001.
- Gary Klein. *Intuition at Work: Why Developing Your Gut Instincts Will Make You Better at What You Do*. New York: Currency Doubleday, 2003.

- Robert J. Kriegel and Louis Patler. *If It Ain't Broke, Break It!* New York: Warner Books, 1991.
- Salvatore Maddi and Deborah Khoshaba. *Resilience at Work: How to Succeed No Matter What Life Throws at You.* New York: AMACOM, 2005.

Articles

- "The Secret of Enduring Greatness," *Fortune,* May 5, 2008. Jim Collins (author of *Good to Great*) addresses the age of turmoil and discusses survivability of corporate stars.
- "The HBR List: Breakthrough Ideas for 2009," *Harvard Business Review,* February 2008. HBR's annual snapshot of the emerging shape of business.
- "The World's Most Admired Companies," *Fortune*, March 29, 2009. *Fortune's* annual list of the most admired companies in the world and why.
- "A Leader's Framework for Decision Making," *Harvard Business Review.* November 2007. Wise executives tailor their approach to fit the complexity of the circumstances they face.
- "Connect and Develop: Inside Procter & Gamble's New Model for Innovation," *Harvard Business Review.* March 2006. For generations, Procter & Gamble generated most of its phenomenal growth by innovating from within, including building global research facilities.
- "Leading Change: Why Transformation Efforts Fail," *Harvard Business Review,* January 2007. Leaders who successfully transform businesses do eight things right (and they do them in the right order).
- "Transcending Business Boundaries: 12,000 World Managers View Change," *Harvard Business Review,* May 2001. The results of the HBR World Leadership Survey found that change is indeed everywhere—regardless of country, culture, or corporation. But the idea of a corporate global village where a common culture of management unifies the practice of business around the world is more dream than reality.
- "What Leaders Really Do," *Harvard Business Review,* December 2001. They don't make plans; they don't solve problems; they don't even organize people. What leaders really do is prepare organizations for change and help them cope as they struggle through it.
- "Meeting the Challenge of Disruptive Change," *Harvard Business Review,* March 2000. It's no wonder that innovation is so difficult for established firms. They

employ highly capable people—and then set them to work within processes and business models that doom them to failure. But there are ways out of this dilemma.

Websites/Blogs

- www.changingminds.org, one of the largest sites in the world on all aspects of how we change what others think, believe, feel, and do. Over 2,500 pages.
- www.margaretwheatley.com. Top female researcher presents her thoughts concerning change.
- www.mariosundar.wordpress.com/2006/07/09/top-10-ceo-blogs/ list of top ten CEO blogs, including Jonathan Schwartz of Sun Microsystems.

HOW THE COACH MODELS THIS PRACTICE

- ◆ Share a story about how you test your own skills as it relates to coaching, for example, if you have invited another coach along to rate you and give you feedback.
- ◆ Explain that your job is to challenge leaders to try new and innovative ways to do their work.
- ◆ Describe what you do to improve your processes, where you've taken classes, perhaps an unusual place you found resources or have reached out to a well-known author for support.
- ◆ Describe your process when things do not go as expected in the partnership. Share an example.
- ◆ Set goals and measurable milestones with your leader.
- ◆ During your coaching, share failures as well as successes with your leader. We learn more from mistakes, ours and others, than we do from doing something right.

CHAPTER 5: COACHING TO ENABLE OTHERS TO ACT

In This Chapter

- Review the Enable Other to Act practice.
- List the corresponding commitments.
- Identify the six LPI items that reference this practice.
- Examine potential questions and activities a coach could use.
- Provide additional resources.
- Consider how the coach could model this practice.

Exemplary leaders know that those who are expected to produce the results must feel a sense of personal power and ownership. Leaders understand that to create a climate that enables others they need to determine what the group needs in order to do its work and to build the team around a common purpose and mutual respect. When leaders Enable Others to Act, they plan how to Foster Collaboration and proactively identify ways to Strengthen Others; they do not leave them to chance.

FOSTER COLLABORATION

Collaboration is a critical competency for achieving and sustaining high performance. In a world that is trying to do more with less, competitive strategies naturally lose to strategies that promote collaboration. With multiple constituencies come diverse and frequently conflicting interests. As paradoxical as it might seem, leadership is more essential when collaboration is required.

World-class performance isn't possible unless there's a strong sense of shared creation and shared responsibility. To Foster Collaboration, leaders must be skilled in two essentials. They must:

- Create a climate of trust
- Facilitate relationships

Create a climate of trust. Trust is at the heart of collaboration. It is the central issue in human relationships. Without trust leaders cannot lead. Without trust leaders cannot get extraordinary things done. Those who are unable to trust others fail to become leaders. Leaders' inability to trust others results in others' lack of trust in them. Leaders know that trusting others pays off; that is why they are the first to trust. Trusting isn't just a way for leaders to foster collaboration; it is healthy for the leader, too. People who are trusting are more likely to be happy and well-adjusted. Trusting leaders nurture openness, involvement, personal satisfaction, and high levels of commitment to excellence. What is the best way to nurture a trusting climate? The best advice is to be the first to trust. Going first requires self-confidence. Trust can't be forced, but it can be nurtured. To demonstrate trust, leaders are open to alternative viewpoints, use others' expertise, are willing to let others exercise influence over group decisions, and share information and resources. Trust is a reciprocal process. Trust is not just what's in your mind; it's also what's in your heart.

Facilitate relationships. To achieve extraordinary things, people have to rely on each other. They need to have a sense of mutual dependence and knowledge and know that they need others to be successful. Leaders create conditions in which people know they can count on each other. Leaders develop cooperative goals and roles, support norms of reciprocity, structure projects to promote joint efforts, and support face-to-face interactions. Leaders know that cooperative goals and roles bind people into cooperative efforts. To facilitate relationships, everyone has a role that supports a goal. Leaders understand that any long-term relationship is built on a sense of reciprocity so that people understand that they will be better off by cooperating. Leaders facilitate relationships through projects that demonstrate that working together is more likely to lead to success than working alone by emphasizing the long-term payoffs. Finally, as everyone becomes more dependent on virtual connections, leaders recognize the importance that face-to-face interactions play in facilitating relationships and fostering collaboration. Virtual trust, like virtual reality, is one step removed from the real thing.

STRENGTHEN OTHERS

Leaders can strengthen others by creating a climate in which people are fully engaged and feel in control of their own lives. People must have the latitude to make decisions based on what they believe should be done. Leaders have to create a climate that both develops others' abilities to complete assignments and builds their self-confidence.

Leaders can significantly increase people's belief in their own ability to make a difference. Leaders can move from being in control to giving over control to others, by becoming their coaches and teachers. They can help others learn new skills and develop existing talents. They can provide the institutional support necessary for ongoing individual growth. The bottom line is that leaders are turning their constituents into leaders.

Creating a climate in which people are fully engaged and feel in control of their own lives is at the heart of strengthening others. People must have the latitude to make decisions, and they must hold themselves personally accountable for the results. This requires that leaders implement two essentials that Strengthen Others:

- Enhance self-determination
- Develop competence and confidence

Enhance self-determination. Self-determined employees have some control over their lives and feel engaged in what they do. Self-determined employees who are more engaged are less likely to look for another job and to miss work. Self-determination can be enhanced in several ways. One of the most significant actions leaders can take is to provide more choices for employees. Employees with choices can make decisions and keep things moving forward when something occurs that is not in the "script." Leaders can also enhance self-determination by designing jobs that offer latitude to ensure that leaders feel as if they are in control of their own work lives. Narrow job categories confine choices; broader categories permit increased flexibility and discretion. Finally, leaders can foster accountability. The more freedom of choice people have, the more responsibility they must accept. Accountability ensures that people feel ownership and are more self-determined to achieve success.

Develop competence and confidence. To get extraordinary things done, leaders must invest in strengthening the capacity and the resolve of everyone in the organization. Without the knowledge, skills, information, and resources to do a job expertly, without feeling competent to skillfully execute choices, people may feel overwhelmed and immobilized. Leaders who expect employees to make good decisions and to accept responsibility for them must also provide training and development, education and coaching. Strengthening Others requires that leaders invest in both formal and informal learning opportunities—training sessions as well as opportunities to share ideas with each other. Leaders must also consider how to organize work to build competence by building in challenges for everyone, enriching jobs by adding variety to each, ensuring that jobs are designed so that people know what is expected of them, and creating opportunities for employees to network with others in the organization. Leaders must foster self-confidence in order to strengthen people. A lack of self-confidence leads to lower aspirations and productivity. And finally, leaders coach, actively seeking ways to increase choice, develop individuals' capabilities, and foster self-confidence.

Enable Others to Act is the practice that encourages leaders to build supportive relationship with all employees on the team. By developing the competence and confidence of the team members in a cooperative environment a team can accomplish extraordinary things. To summarize, the two commitments aligned to Enable Others to Act include:

- **Commitment 7:** Foster collaboration by building trust and facilitating relationships.
- **Commitment 8:** Strengthen others by increasing self-determination and developing competence.

Enable Others to Act is as powerful as doubling the size of an organization. Leaders foster collaboration and strengthen others to be more involved, engaged, and accountable. Leaders make it possible for others to do good work.

ENABLE OTHERS TO ACT: PRACTICE FOR THE LPI ITEMS

The following six statements refer to the items in the *LPI: Leadership Practices Inventory* that relate to Enable Others to Act. The numbers reference the item number in the LPI. These items are numbered and listed in the order as they appear in the LPI. This is done to make it easy to locate each item in this book; the order in which the items are discussed in this book does not suggest an order of importance.

You need to determine, based on your client's feedback, which items your client wants to work on and in what sequence.

After each item, you will find suggested questions and activities. These are created for a coaching situation and may be used with the leader(s) you may be coaching. Several of the activities reference a "journal." There is an assumption that your leader will have a personal journal in which to track plans, questions, and desires. A journal is an important tool for reflection on a leader's journey to excellence.

Note: There are many more activities than you would ever use with one person. Work with your client to identify one that will be most useful. Even better, have your clients create their own after you present some possibilities. Remember, the value of these activities and discussion questions is not in the doing, but in the follow-on discussion with you, the coach. Be sure to allow time to discuss the "so what" and the "now what" that occur as a result of any discussion or activity.

At the end of this chapter you will find a resource list that includes books, articles, websites, and blogs for you or your client to use. You will also find a section titled "How the Coach Models This Practice," which serves as a reminder to you about what you must do to be a positive, proactive model for your client.

4. I develop cooperative relationships among the people I work with.

Questions You Can Ask

- How do you interpret this item?
- Why is developing cooperative relationships important?
- What are the key relationships that you should nurture in order to be successful in your job?
- How would you describe the relationships you have with most of your people?
- Does anyone on your team require more attention than others and if so, who? How do you manage that relationship?
- What struggles has your team been through that have made cooperation difficult?
- How do you let people in on who you are?
- How do you build trust with the people you work with?
- Imagine that you have a model team. What does it look like? What is it doing? What are you doing?

- What is preventing you from developing cooperative relationships with everyone on the team?
- How do you balance competition with cooperation in your team?

Activities You Can Suggest

- **Partner with Me:** List up to five individuals with whom you believe you should partner on a sustained basis. What is your current relationship with these individuals? Rate your relationship using the following scale:
  1. Non-existent.
  2. Limited partnering opportunities.
  3. I have access and could partner on a general basis.
  4. We have an excellent relationship and true reasons to partner for tactical as well as strategic reasons that will benefit the team and/or the organization.

  If you rated anyone a "1," determine what you can do to build the partnership and recognize that you will need to take the first step. If you rated anyone as a "2" or "3," it will be easier to gain access to him or her, but you must still determine ways to move the relationship up to the next level. And if you have rated someone as a "4"—what are you waiting for?

- **Ponder This Quote:** John Madden said, "Coaches have to watch for what they don't want to see and listen for what they don't want to hear." When building relationships, you need to watch for what you don't want to see and listen for what you don't want to hear. Make a list of items that you have heard and seen recently that you know need to be addressed in order to build your relationships.

- **Weekly Staff Meetings:** It may seem simple, but be sure you are having weekly—well run—staff meetings that bring everyone together and up-to-speed. How can you get the most from your staff meetings? Can you begin with a personal, relationship-building question, such as, "What book are you reading this summer?" Invite your team members to take turns leading the meetings.

- **Caution Your Tongue:** Take care with your communication to ensure that it is continually building relationships. One of the greatest derailments of potentially successful leaders is that they speak destructively about their companies, their management, or other team members without thinking about the results. If you are guilty of this major blunder, make changes quickly in this area. How? You need to change a bad habit and turn it around. Before talking about someone else, get in the habit of asking yourself four questions before speaking:

1. Will this comment help our company?
2. Will this comment help our customers?
3. Will this comment help the person with whom I am talking?
4. Will this comment help the person about whom I am speaking?

If you cannot answer yes to all four questions, don't say it. There is a big difference between being honest and candid and gossiping destructively. After reading this activity, ask one of your co-workers or your supervisor or even one of your direct reports to observe your communication for a week. At the end of the week, take the person to lunch and ask for his or her observations—especially about those comments or behaviors that could be destructive. Practice good listening skills.

- **Future Leader Relationships:** Developing and maintaining relationships inside the organization includes a special focus on your relationships with future leaders. The individuals who have been tapped as high-potential employees, likely future leaders for the organization, are special people with whom you will want to go out of your way to initiate and maintain a relationship. Accepting your responsibility in developing and maintaining these special relationships encourages them to stay with the organization. You will be helping the organization retain this unique talent pool. High-potential employees are a corporate asset. Do what you can to retain this asset.

- **Check Yourself:** Create a checklist for yourself. Make a list of things you believe help initiate, develop, and maintain relationships. Literally thousands of items could be placed on this checklist. You will have a sense of what is important for you to improve this skill. After you've created an initial list, you may want to take it back to your coach or have someone whom you trust review it to provide insight about other things that you could add. To start you might consider these:

  - Listen without judging.
  - Understand other people and where they come from.
  - Take the first step to get to know others better.
  - Initiate conversations—have a list of discussion starters available.
  - Learn three non-work items about everyone: hobbies, children, interests, or others.
  - Treat people equitably; but remember, different people have different needs.

- Share something about yourself.
- Practice reliability and accountability.
- **Power of the Unexpected:** Building your emotional connections with team members develops and maintains relationships. This is important because it enhances trust and boosts retention. Unexpected reinforcing connections can be very powerful. Find ways to surprise your direct reports, co-workers, peers, even your boss! Here are a few ideas to consider:
  - Invite a team member to breakfast or lunch and ask what matters most to him or her and what you can do as a leader to support the future dream.
  - Send a greeting card to a spouse or significant other stating the value the person brings to the organization.
  - Plan an outing to a local event, theme park, fishing trip, or picnic for your team. Invite families when appropriate.
  - Arrange for senior management to share corporate goals with all the staff in an impromptu meeting the next time someone visits your organization.
  - Bring in some homemade food—something you've made such as cookies or candy—for no special occasion.

  Ask a team member to plan one of these with you to encourage his or her involvement.
- **Words Get in the Way:** Sometimes what we say isn't what we meant to say. Ask someone who works with you on a daily basis to observe what you say and how you say it. Could your communication be misinterpreted in any way? For example, do you have a strange sense of humor that may not be seen as humor all the time? Trying to be candid may appear to be an excuse. For example, saying, "I've never been very organized" may appear to be an excuse for not completing your work. Sometimes *how* you say something may prevent good communication. For example, do you become overly excited when something goes wrong? Instead use positive non-verbals: nod when someone speaks, smile appropriately, don't check your watch, and be attentive.
- **Fit It in Every Day:** Find ways to fit in building relationships every day. Try a couple of these:
  - Walk the halls—slowly—stopping to chat with whomever you see.
  - Fill your water glass at the same water cooler with everyone else and strike up a discussion with others.
  - Eat lunch and take your breaks in the same places that your employees do.
  - Keep your door open.

- Invite small groups to go to lunch with you.
- Display trust of others.

- **Resolve a Conflict:** Sometimes relationships go awry and it appears that nothing you do can get them back on track again. If this is the case, you may ask your coach or supervisor to become involved. You could attempt various things. You might ask your coach or supervisor to serve as a sounding board for you. You might also ask him or her to be an intermediary to meditate the issue. Go into these sessions being willing to give more than 50 percent. If the other person sees that you are willing to submit, there is a greater likelihood that he or she will be willing to do it as well. Compromise is much easier to reach if everyone is willing to share the blame.

- **What Would Your Friends Say?** Take a friend out to coffee and share that you want to learn to be better at initiating and building relationships. Generally, our friends like us no matter who we are. They overlook our weaknesses. Ask your friend to identify the blocks you may have to building relationships. Keep a list of them and begin to see them as improvement opportunities. Develop them at work.

- **Build Your Team:** When was the last time you took your team offsite to conduct team building? Annually is not too often. Bring in a neutral facilitator and use the time away to work on issues and resolve difficult problems your team is facing. You build the team, get away from the day-to-day grind, and solve problems. What a great use of time!

- **Trust—Key to Good Communication:** Building a strong foundation of trust is one of the quickest ways to establish good communication and show confidence in others. It's hard to tell which comes first—trust or confidence. Listed here are actions that you can take to build trust. Rate yourself on these actions. How consistent are you? If any of these skills need to be improved, begin today.
  - Ensure that your words and actions are congruent; avoid mixed messages.
  - Act in ways that support the values of your organization.
  - When having difficulty with a co-worker or team member, go directly to that individual to discuss the situation. Be a straight shooter, discussing issues with that person rather than with others about the person.
  - Be a sounding board on sensitive issues for others. Demonstrate strong listening capability.
  - Share your own opinions and perspectives, even when they are different from the majority view. Avoid being a "yes" person.

- Keep your focus on the big picture and the shared goals of the organization.
- Accept accountability for your own actions and the results of those actions.
- Avoid blaming others. Instead focus on what can be done to fix any difficult situation.
- **Be Neighborly:** Work to mend relations with a difficult neighbor. Taking the first step toward reconciliation often is just what is needed to continue discussions.

9. I actively listen to diverse points of view.

Questions You Can Ask

- How do you rate your listening skills?
- What prevents you from rating your listening skills at the highest level?
- Think of a time when you were a perfect listener. What were the circumstances surrounding that situation?
- How accepting do you think you are of diverse points of view? Can you provide me with examples?
- What are your blind spots in this area?
- If your team rated how well you supported diverse opinions, how well would you do?
- What do you do when you hear two opposite points of view?
- What are the advantages and disadvantages of having a diverse team?
- How would you describe the broadest diversity on your team, and how do you manage it?

Activities You Can Suggest

- **Active Listening:** Go to www.mindtools.com/CommSkll/ActiveListening.htm and jot down notes about how to be an active listener. Sit down with your spouse, significant other, or best friend. Tell the person that you would like some honest and candid feedback about your listening skills. Then listen, listen, listen. Practice the active listening skills identified on the website.
  - Pay attention.
  - Show that you are listening.
  - Provide feedback.

- Defer judgment.
- Respond appropriately.

Do not interrupt. Do not say, "yes, but." Do not make excuses. Be sure to ask for suggestions about how you could be a better listener. Accept the feedback graciously and begin to put into practice all that you heard.

- **Listening Leader:** Let your supervisor know that you would like to offer to be a problem solver for employees. During off hours you would like to make yourself available to anyone who would like to talk to someone in a leadership position in the organization. The discussions will be held in strictest confidence. Obtain advice and suggestions from your supervisor. This is great practice to listen without judgment.

- **Post an Idea:** Looking for ideas to solve a nagging problem? Hang a chart on the wall and begin a mind map. (If you don't know what a mind map is, check Wikipedia's description at http://en.wikipedia.org/wiki/Mind_map.) Post the problem in a circle in the center of a large piece of chart paper. Add a couple of ideas around the outside and place them inside circles also. Draw lines to connect these circles to the larger one in the center. Hang a marker nearby to encourage ideas and input. After a week or so, bring your team together to discuss the ideas. Your job is to listen to the ideas.

- **Reading Material:** Subscribe to *Diversity Inc.* magazine. You can check out their website at www.DiversityInc.com. Contact the human resources or diversity office at your organization to find out whether someone currently receives the electronic version.

- **Form Diverse Teams for Diverse Ideas:** When forming a team, always remember to select the most diverse-thinking individuals. It is the best way to find the best ideas. It is also the best way to model this skill.

- **Bring Your Hobby to Work Day:** Invite everyone on your team to bring a display of his or her hobby (or a picture if that is not possible—if it's hang gliding, for example)—to work on one particular day. Find a location for the displays. Encourage time to share information among individuals. This accomplishes several positive things for your team: (1) it displays the diversity among the group; (2) it demonstrates the creativity, skills, knowledge, and competence within the group; (3) it exhibits the unique ability that each has to provide input from a diverse perspective; (4) it creates an expectation of success when you consider tapping into everyone on the team; and (5) everyone gets to know other team members on a personal basis. ***Important:*** Everyone must participate; leaving anyone out appears exclusionary.

- **Reverse Mentoring:** Implement a reverse mentoring program. The concept is that anyone under twenty-five will mentor anyone over fifty. This could be a one-time program or ongoing. Senior leaders who put themselves into a mentoring situation could learn a great deal about the younger generation. They might even learn to program their flat screen TVs at home. You may also base this on generations, for example, Gen Ys mentoring Baby Boomers. This could also be women or minorities mentoring white male leaders.

- **Obtaining Input and Ideas:** Ask a friend who works at a different company (any industry) to discuss how his or her company encourages input and ideas from diverse perspectives. Ask what role leaders in positions like yours play in this effort. Ask what works and what does not work. Ask how important diversity and inclusion are in the other company. Relate this to your organization and identify how you can incorporate this information into your efforts toward self-development.

14. I treat others with dignity and respect.

Questions You Can Ask

- What actions demonstrate that you are acting with dignity and respect?
- What results when you treat others with dignity and respect?
- What are the opposites of dignity and respect?
- How do individuals' personal styles get in the way of being respectful? Does this ever happen on your team?
- What do you think you need to do to manage this behavior better?
- Imagine that everyone on your team believed that they were respected by everyone else on the team, including you. What would have to happen to reach that point?
- In what way can you give visibility to all members of your team, such as connecting them with others in the organization?

Activities You Can Suggest

- **Take a Stand on Stereotypes:** Few people have the courage to speak out against words and comments that hurt others. Demeaning comments, stereotypes, and bias have no place in today's organizations. Yet they show up in the form of jokes, stories, instructions, cartoons, and other instances in the workplace. Unfortunately, these attitudes and behaviors prevent true teamwork and inclusion in your organization. As a leader in the organization, it is your responsibility to speak up when you hear slurs or even subtle comments. You can simply say, "I feel uncomfortable with that comment (statement, remark, word, name, etc.)." Think about why you may not have taken a stand in the past. Make a pledge to yourself and the organization to do so in the future.

- **Ponder This Quote:** Anne McCaffrey, author, stated, "Make no judgments where you have no compassion." What does this quote mean? What lesson does it hold about initiating, developing, and maintaining relationships? Treating others with dignity and respect? What does it mean personally to you?

- **Inclusion in Our Organization:** Analyze the current inclusion environment in your organization. Use the following questions to start:
  - What are we doing currently to encourage ideas from everyone?
  - What are some outcomes of obtaining input and ideas from our entire team?
  - What worked well to get these ideas?
  - What are our possible roadblocks to really listening to these ideas?
  - How well do we respect others' ideas?
  - What could we do to be more respectful?

  Ask other team members to consider these questions and meet with them to discuss how you are doing and what you could do better.

- **Understanding My Reactions to Others:** Our personal beliefs come from experiences and situations from our pasts, such as home, family, church, television, personal experiences, or our friends. They result in assumptions, biases, and prejudices. Once we internalize them, they become our truths—what we believe. They may become the basis for our beliefs about diversity and inclusion. Take time to explore where your beliefs come from. Identify five or six sources of your biases, prejudices, and assumptions. Circle the ones that have had the greatest impact on you and on your current opinions. Now define how these opinions impact your interactions with others. How can you use what you have learned to create an environment of acceptance and open-mindedness within your team? Put a plan together for what you can do to address this within yourself. Expand your plan to address it within your team.

- **Reach Out for Support:** If you have tried numerous things to create an environment of acceptance and open-mindedness and you are still mired in a negative environment, link up with someone in another department that has a positive working environment. You may also contact someone in your human resources or diversity office. Ask for ideas and resources. Consider inviting the individual to visit and observe your department. Ask for suggestions for what you can do. Implement those ideas.

- **Welcome New Employees:** Create a team that explores creative ways to welcome new team members to expand the climate of acceptance from the first day. Select a diverse team that includes people who have been around for different lengths of time. Be sure to include those who are relatively new so that they can share from recent memory things that would have been nice to have (lists of people, terminology used in the organization, acronyms, even pictures of specific people). The team can use this information to identify ways that people can feel more accepted and welcomed. Meet with your team several times. Present your supervisor with an implementation timeline, plan, and budget.
- **Attend a Course:** If working with diverse groups continues to be an issue in your team, it is worth the investment to take a course. Work with your supervisor and your training department to find the right one.
- **Foster Inclusion from the Start:** Ask your team to brainstorm ways to help new team members feel included right from the start. Some ideas include:
  - Find connections, such as school or friends, to bring a new hire into the discussion immediately.
  - Ask them about their experiences at their last places of employment.
  - Based on the hiring data, use their strengths early.
  - Find out something they have in common with other team members.
- **Understanding the Defining Moments:** Complete this exercise with your team members to help them understand what it feels like when you don't "fit in." Plan on about twenty to forty minutes, depending on the size of your group and the length of the discussion. Begin by sharing a time when you felt "different" or did not fit in with a group. Pair team members up and tell them to share their own situations and how they felt at the time. After five minutes (you may wish to give a half-time signal so that both have time), ask for a couple volunteers to share their situations with the entire group. Use the following questions to start discussion:
  - How did you feel when the situation occurred?
  - How did you feel while telling your story? Why do you think that may have occurred?
  - What did you learn about these kinds of situations?

- How does this relate to the culture and atmosphere we are trying to create in the organization?
- What will you do differently as a result of this experience?

You may wish to point out that even those in the majority have experienced feelings of being "different." Being perceived as different creates negative feelings that often linger after the incident is over. If the feelings occur often enough, it leads to misunderstanding of others' behavior. Encourage everyone to remember their own feelings the next time they are in a group in which someone may feel "different."

- **Join Organizations:** Identify an organization in which you would be in the minority. Stretch and grow your learning edges. What ideas does this give you for what you can do to treat others with dignity and respect?

19. I involve people in the decisions that directly impact their job performance.

Questions You Can Ask

- Describe how you involve people in decisions.
- What happens when the decision is the wrong one—perhaps it leads to rework, errors, loss of profits, increased stress?
- What if you made all the decisions?
- What types of decisions impact people's job performance? What concerns do you have about being taken advantage of?
- What types of decisions do you feel your team members would like to be a part of?
- How does a team member conclude that he or she should or should not make a decision?
- What are you giving up when you allow people to make decisions that impact their job performance?
- How can you build reliability and predictability into the way your team members make decisions?
- How can you give your power away to strengthen your team members?

Activities You Can Suggest

- **I Wouldn't Do It That Way:** Experiencing decisions that are different from yours is a form of accepting a change. Everyone responds differently to doing things differently—changing. Some are excited about change. Some dread it. Some just go along with it because there's nothing much that can be done anyway. Your attitude about change is important as a leader. How you react to change determines the impact change will have on you. No one controls how you respond to change—just you. Think about the last change you went through—personal or work-related.

- What did you think?
- How did you feel about the change?
- What happened that made the change difficult or easy?
- What do you think you did well?
- What do you wish you had done differently?

Now think about what happens when someone makes a decision that is different from your decision. Same reaction? How do you wish you could react instead? Role play several situations with your supervisor, a colleague, or your coach.

- **More Responsibility:** Find ways to continuously give your employees more and more responsibility. This will both prepare them and encourage them to make more and better-informed decisions and changes that lead to doing their work better or faster.

- **Pick Me!** To build self-esteem and help employees feel good about making decisions, assign all tasks to employees. Spread the responsibility around. Don't always assign the difficult, important, high priorities to the same people. Allow everyone to learn and grow. The better informed they are, the more experiences they have, the more skilled they will be at making decisions.

- **Show Me the Money:** Next time you need to promote an idea to a co-worker or an employee, lead with the outcome you desire: "Show me the money" *Jerry Maguire* style. Begin by stating what you want the outcome to be up-front. Then turn it over to your employee to make a decision about how to do the job. What are you promoting? What should it look like when complete? Formulate a plan. Decide on your complete message. Write it down. Then meet with the person and tell him or her what needs to be done. Improved communication helps your employee take on a successful project.

- **Spur-of-the-Moment Cautions:** Sometimes you do not have time to think about whether to support or deny an idea or decision. Meet with a co-worker to brainstorm a list of how you might be better prepared when these situations arise. Keep your list for future use. For example, even though it might appear to be time-sensitive, can it actually wait for fifteen minutes while you weigh the pros and cons and organize your thoughts? How does it correlate to the organization's vision? Your responses should always build esteem and never put anyone down.

- **Knowing When to Hold 'em and When to Fold 'em:** Knowing when to speak up and when to let it go is critical. Meet with your supervisor or coach and ask for guidance from his or her experience. Think through your own situations in which you have to respond. What are the two or three key thoughts you can keep in mind? Write them in your journal.
- **Critical Thinking:** Consider taking a critical thinking class. The American Management Association offers one that is practical and useful. Your training department can help you track it down or visit the organization's website to read more about the course content.

24. I give people a great deal of freedom and choice in deciding how to do their work.

Questions You Can Ask

- What does this behavior mean to you?
- How do you give your team members discretion and autonomy in their specific jobs?
- Describe how you complete this behavior. What are some examples? How would your team describe this behavior?
- How does your team address differences that naturally occur when one person's choice is not the best for all, for example, one person changes his or her process and this prevents another from doing his or her job on time?
- Why do you think this behavior is or is not important to your team?
- To what extent would your team members say they are encouraged to use their personal strengths in the workplace?
- What do you do that provides the guidance so that individuals can make good decisions?
- How do team members hold themselves accountable?
- What prevents your team members from making good decisions in how to do their work?

Activities You Can Suggest

- **Decision-Making Tools:** In order for your employees to have choices about doing their work, they need to know several ways to make decisions. Go to www .mindtools.com and click on the Decision Making section. Review the various ways to make decisions. The website displays techniques that use Pareto analysis, paired comparison analysis, grid analysis, decision trees, PMI, force field analysis, Six Thinking Hats®, and cost/benefit analysis. It also offers an explanation for how and when to use each. Invite your employees to visit the same website to examine the decision-making tools. Get together and identify the advantages and disadvantages of each method. Discuss when each tool would be the most useful. Encourage them to use the tools to make choices about how to do their work.

- **Be Curious:** Questions are a magical way to initiate a discussion and to build a relationship. Have you ever gone to a party and found that a well-posed question opens the door for others to talk? In fact, often people will say you provided the most interesting conversation when, in fact, you didn't say a word; you just listened. If you are not spontaneously conversant, plan your questions ahead. What curiosity questions could you ask that could begin a solid conversation that encourages your employees to make choices about how they do their work? When successful, this will also continue to build your relationship. Here are a few question starters:
  - How do you see . . . ?
  - What if we . . . ?
  - What do you think about . . . ?
  - How do you believe we could . . . ?
  - Have you ever . . . ?

  These question starters about an employee's work show that you are interested in his or her ideas. Ask more questions than other people. You will build more relationships.

- **Stretch Them:** Identify stretch assignments for your team members to help them learn what is important in doing the work. Stretch assignments are those opportunities that are just outside the individual's area of expertise and comfort zone that stretch and enhance his or her skill set.

- **Direct Report Discussions:** Schedule periodic individual discussions with your direct reports to set long-term goals, take things off their plates, review their career goals, answer their questions, provide feedback, review their development plans, and ensure they are making progress in the direction they would like. Encourage them to find new ways to improve how they do their work.

29. I ensure that people grow in their jobs by learning new skills and developing themselves.

Questions You Can Ask

- What does this mean and why is it important?
- How do you determine what individuals need in order to grow in their jobs? How does this relate to the entire organization?
- What kinds of things have you done that demonstrate this behavior?
- What issues do you face that prevent you from doing what you would like to do to grow your team members?
- How do you determine who to assign tasks to on your team? Is that the best way to ensure that everyone has an opportunity to develop?
- What if you did this behavior right? What would happen?
- What are the most important skills required of your team?
- How do you ensure that you grow in your job?

Activities You Can Suggest

- **Become a Mentor:** Become a mentor and two people learn. One of the best ways to learn more yourself is to become a mentor to another person. Your protégé will bring up topics, ask questions, pose challenges, and tell you things that will force you to learn more about leadership. Being a mentor also keeps you in tune to what is occurring in other areas of the organization and with the people who are a level or two down the management chain. What did you learn as a mentor that you can transfer to your team to ensure that team members grow?
- **Teach a Teammate:** Let it be known that you would like to teach team members new skills. The act of teaching reinforces your need to hone the skills. In addition, teaching improves your communication skills and helps you to identify other skills that you may need to improve, for example, logical thinking or clearer conversation delivery.
- **Take Note:** Keep a pocket notebook and pen with you at all times. Observe others on your team throughout the day. As you see opportunities for coaching

and development, make a note. At the end of each day, review what you have written in your notebook. Decide how you can implement each of your ideas, whether you can combine the developmental requirements of several employees, how to locate the resources to implement the development required, and what else you need to do to cultivate the full potential of each of your team members. Use your notebook diligently.

- **Developmental Buddy:** While identifying developmental ideas for your team members, consider how you and a co-worker in another department could work together. For example, could you trade employees for a short time period to give each of them a new developmental experience? Could you provide a learning/training opportunity for several employees from both of your teams at the same time? Could you share ideas for the "problem" employees that you each may have? Could you act as sounding boards for each other as you look for new and exciting opportunities to develop employees? Find a "Developmental Buddy" with whom to exchange ideas and concerns. One positive consequence is that it will enhance your development as well!

- **Extra Experience:** Tap one or more of your promising team members to work with you on a community project. Perhaps you have decided to support a "Clean Up the Bay Day" or you are volunteering in a soup kitchen for a day. Invite team members along to provide them with an opportunity to have a different set of experiences and perhaps to take a leadership role. This will also give you an opportunity to see them in another setting.

- **Mentor a Student:** Coaching and mentoring are leadership tasks. Practice your mentoring, coaching, and leadership skills by volunteering to mentor a high school student. Check with your local school system for more information.

- **Volunteer to Develop Others:** Many organizations would welcome your skills to develop others. Check with your local Boys Club, Girls Club, Big Brother, Big Sister, 4-H, Boy Scouts, Girl Scouts, or other locally supported civic groups.

- **Shadow Learner:** Invite one of your employees to shadow you for a day. During breaks, take time to explain what you are doing and why. Remember, what is common sense to you may seem unusual to someone else. Be sure to invite questions. Finally, ask whether the person is interested in developing the skills required to move into a management position.

- **Retain Your Top Performers:** Retention is a concern for all organizations. It is always important to engage employees to keep turnover down. The pursuit of career goals and personal development consistently tops the list of reasons why employees leave a job. A key aspect of controlling retention is to figure out what motivates and inspires top performers to stay. Offering support, especially to top performers you want to retain, is key and affects the bottom line. Unfortunately, top performers often believe that they need to consider other employers to advance their careers. Develop a plan to ensure that you retain top performers. Your plan should answer these questions:

- How can I ensure our top performers realize that they can have careers with this organization?
- What topics can I discuss with employees that excite them about the work and the organization?
- How can I involve employees in solving problems?
- What opportunities can I provide that offer change and challenge?
- What discussion can I pursue about the organization's vision?
- What investment can I make in developing top performers?
- How can I foster desirable turnover, for example, aggressive supervisors and low performers?
- Am I doing all that I can to support boomerang employees (those who will leave but will come back again)?

These questions address the reasons that most people stay at an organization: career opportunities, inspiration, accomplishing something of value, opportunity to make a difference, challenging work, exciting future, developmental opportunities, feeling valued, and feeling supported. This kind of support will not go unnoticed by either your top performers or your manager.

- **Meeting Tag Along:** Invite one of your up-and-coming employees to observe a meeting for managers or department heads. After the meeting, discuss what happened and answer any questions your employee may have.
- **Employee Engagement:** Retaining a productive, competent workforce is an important challenge to leaders. Stay on your toes at all times to determine what you can do to engage employees so they will want to stay. Google "Employee Engagement" on the web. Follow several of the links. Don't stop until you have two solid ideas about what you could do to motivate and inspire others and engage them so they will want to remain with the organization.
- **A Good Book and a Cuppa Joe:** Invite one of your promising employees to visit a local book store with you (preferably one that serves coffee). Find books that influenced you as a leader. Pull them from the shelves. Over cups of coffee or tea, review with your employee the important lessons you learned from each book.

- **Coach Me, Coach You:** Use what you are learning from your coaching experience and put it into use with your own team. What can you do to coach each of your team members? Plan a regular schedule of meetings. Find out what they would like to improve, establish goals, and then challenge, encourage, and reinforce them to success.

BOOKS AND ARTICLES

Books for Enable Others to Act

- Michael Abrashoff. *It's Your Ship: Management Techniques from the Best Damn Ship in the Navy*. New York: Warner, 2002.
- Elaine Biech. *10 Steps to Successful Training*. Alexandria, VA: ASTD Press, 2008.
- Ken Blanchard, John Carlos, and Alan Randolph. *The Three Keys to Empowerment*. San Francisco: Berrett-Koehler, 1999.
- Leigh Branham. *The Seven Hidden Reasons Employees Leave: How to Recognize the Subtle Signs and Act Before It's Too Late*. New York: AMACOM, 2005.
- Hyler Bracey. *Building Trust: How to Get It! How to Keep It!* Taylorsville, GA: HR Artworks, 2002.
- Warren Bennis and Patricia Ward Biederman. *Organizing Genius: The Secrets of Creative Collaboration*. Reading, MA: Addison-Wesley, 1997.
- Peter Block. *The Empowered Manager: Positive Political Skills at Work*. San Francisco: Jossey-Bass, 1987.
- Marcus Buckingham and Curt Coffman. *First, Break All the Rules: What the World's Greatest Managers Do Differently*. New York: Simon & Schuster, 1999.
- Cary Cherniss and Daniel Goleman (Eds.). *The Emotionally Intelligent Workplace: How to Select for, Measure, and Improve Emotional Intelligence in Individuals, Groups, and Organizations*. San Francisco: Jossey-Bass, 2001.
- Robert B. Cialdini. *Influence: How and Why People Agree to Things*. New York: Quill, 1984.
- Steven M.R. Covey with Rebecca R. Merrill. *The Speed of Trust: The One Thing That Changes Everything*. New York: The Free Press, 2006.
- Roger Fisher and William Ury. *Getting to Yes*. New York: Penguin, 1988.
- Daniel Goleman. *Working with Emotional Intelligence*. New York: Bantam, 1998.
- Daniel Goleman, Richard Boyatzis, and Annie McKee. *Primal Leadership: Realizing the Power of Emotional Intelligence*. Boston: Harvard Business School Press, 2002.

- Malcolm Gladwell. *The Tipping Point: How Little Things Make a Big Difference.* Boston: Little, Brown, 2002.
- Patrick Lencioni. *The Five Dysfunctions of a Team: A Field Guide for Leaders, Managers, and Facilitators.* San Francisco: Jossey-Bass, 2005.
- Patrick Lencioni. *The Five Dysfunctions of a Team: Participant Workbook.* San Francisco: Wiley, 2012.
- Patrick Lencioni. *Overcoming The Five Dysfunctions of a Team: A Leadership Fable.* San Francisco: Jossey-Bass, 2002.
- Charles A. O'Reilly and Jeffrey Pfeffer. *Hidden Value: How Great Companies Achieve Extraordinary Results with Ordinary People.* Boston: Harvard Business School Press, 2000.
- Tom Rath. *Vital Friends: The People You Can't Afford to Live Without.* New York: Gallup Press, 2006.
- Dennis Reina and Michelle Reina. *Trust and Betrayal in the Workplace: Building Effective Relationships in Your Organization.* San Francisco: Berrett-Koehler, 2006.
- Tim Sanders. *The Likeability Factor: How to Boost Your L-Factor and Achieve Your Life's Dreams.* New York: HarperCollins, 2006.
- Robert Shaw. *Trust in the Balance: Building Successful Organizations on Results, Integrity, and Concern.* San Francisco: Jossey-Bass, 1997.
- Jack Stack and Bo Burlingham. *A Stake in the Outcome: Building a Culture of Ownership for the Long-Term Success of Your Business.* New York: Currency Doubleday, 2002.
- James Surowiecki. *The Wisdom of Crowds: Why the Many Are Smarter Than the Few and How Collective Wisdom Shapes Business, Economies, Societies, and Nations.* New York: Anchor Books, 2005.
- Rodd Wagner and Gale Muller. *Power of 2: Make the Most of Your Partnerships at Work and in Life.* Washington, DC: Gallup Press, 2009.

Articles

- "Manage Your Energy, Not Your Time," *Harvard Business Review,* October 2007. The science of stamina has advanced to the point where individuals, teams, and whole organizations can, with some straightforward interventions, significantly increase their capacity to get things done.
- "Developing Your Leadership Pipeline," *Harvard Business Review,* October 2005. Succession planning and leadership development ought to be two sides of the

same coin. So why do many companies manage them as if they had nothing to do with each other?

- "Why Employer Brand Is Critical to Retention and Engagement," *Talent Management* magazine, May 2008. An employer's brand should be as clear, relevant, and exciting as its consumer brand. If done right, it aids recruiting and retention efforts and creates brand ambassadors who spread the good word and bring in top talent.
- "Thinking Like a CEO," *Talent Management* magazine, September 2007. The trend toward talent management has increased how employee performance and workplace practices affect the bottom line. But some doubt that talent managers can effectively step into this more strategic role. To earn the C-suite's respect, talent managers need to look at the business as a whole and think like the CEO.
- "Eight Ways to Build Collaborative Teams," *Harvard Business Review,* November 2007. Even the largest and most complex teams can work together effectively if the right conditions are in place.
- "Women and the Labyrinth of Leadership," *Harvard Business Review,* September 2007. When you put all the pieces together, a new picture emerges for why women don't make it into the C-suite. It's not the glass ceiling, but the sum of many obstacles along the way.
- "The Ethical Mind: A Conversation with Psychologist Howard Gardner," *Harvard Business Review,* March 2007. It's not enough to espouse high standards. To live up to them—and help others do the same—requires an ethical cast of mind that lets you practice your principles consistently.
- "Rethinking Political Correctness," *Harvard Business Review,* September 2006. Sensitivity to race, religion, or gender is a good thing, but too often it is driven by fear. Rather than walk on eggshells, managers can learn to develop more productive, meaningful relationships at work.

HOW THE COACH MODELS THIS PRACTICE

- Go beyond developing a cooperative relationship with your leaders.
- Use your active listening skills at all times, especially when it is difficult to listen to an opinion that you know is not a good leadership practice. It is your job to help your leader see the other perspective.

- Treating your leaders with dignity and respect is Coaching 101. View your leaders as partners, respect their opinions, and look for their strengths.

- Right from the start, allow your leaders to decide how they want to build their leadership capacity. They will decide what they want to work on and how they will do it. You are there to act as a sounding board, provide suggestions and ideas, give encouragement, and celebrate their successes. A good coach knows that leaders have the right decisions within them.

- Provide lots of choices. This book, for example, provides lists of ideas, although you will probably need to customize them for your leaders. Offer ideas, not solutions. Your leader will know best about how to make improvements in his or her situation.

- The entire coaching process ensures that your leaders grow by learning new skills. Track the skills that are most important to your leaders and encourage them to continuously look for ways to develop themselves.

CHAPTER 6: COACHING TO ENCOURAGE THE HEART

In This Chapter

- Review the Encourage the Heart practice.
- List the corresponding commitments.
- Identify the six LPI items that reference this practice.
- Examine potential questions and activities a coach could use.
- Provide additional resources.
- Consider how the coach could model this practice.

Achieving success in this ever-changing fast-paced world is difficult. Leaders know that they must Encourage the Heart of their constituents to carry on. Genuine acts of caring uplift the spirits and draw people forward. This practice is important because it brings the team together, it improves communication, and it builds a strong coalition that can address almost any issue or concern. It gives team members satisfaction for a job well done, and it gives leaders closure on a specific action, a larger milestone, or even the final product. Leaders who Encourage the Heart ensure that they Recognize Contributions and Celebrate Values and Victories.

RECOGNIZE CONTRIBUTIONS

Recognition is about acknowledging good results and reinforcing positive performance. It's about shaping an environment in which everyone's contributions are noticed and appreciated. In high-performing organizations, people work quite intensely and often put in long hours, but this doesn't mean that leaders should not take the time to provide recognition. People need emotional fuel to replenish their spirits. They need the will to continue and recognition by the leader to boost their morale.

Leaders who understand the critical need to Recognize Contributions stimulate and motivate the internal drive within each individual. To accomplish this, leaders must be engaged in these essentials:

- Expect the best
- Personalize recognition

Expect the best. Successful leaders have high expectations of themselves and of their constituents. These expectations are powerful because people tend to live up to a leader's expectations. Exemplary leaders get high performance because they believe in the abilities of their constituents. They set high expectations because they know that they're more likely to achieve high performance if they expect high performance. This is referred to as the Pygmalion effect. Leaders are clear about what's expected of people and what they are trying to accomplish. This helps people stay the course and reach the goal. Goals give recognition a context, allowing people to be recognized for achieving something, for doing something extraordinary. Leaders ensure that people know whether they're making progress toward the goal by providing feedback. When leaders provide a clear sense of direction and feedback along the way, they encourage people to reach inside and do their best.

Personalize recognition. When people recall their most meaningful recognition, they consistently say that it's "personal." By personalizing recognition, leaders send the message that someone took the time to notice the achievement, seek out the responsible individual, and personally deliver praise in a timely manner. Personalized recognition requires four things of a leader. First, leaders must get close to people; they need to know their constituents. This also enhances trust, and people are more willing to follow someone they like and trust. Second, leaders must be creative about incentives and not rely exclusively on the organization's formal reward system. Often simple personal gestures are the most powerful rewards. Third, just say "thank you." None of us make enough use of this powerful two-word reward that goes a long way in sustaining high performance. Fourth, leaders need to be thoughtful, and that requires knowing enough about the other person to make the recognition memorable. All of these lead to the ability to provide memorable personalized recognition.

CELEBRATE VALUES AND VICTORIES

All over the world, in every culture, people stop working on certain days and take time to celebrate. We hold parades, cheer champions, set off fireworks, or attend banquets to respect accomplishments of individuals and groups. Why do we take time away from work to come together, tell stories, and raise our spirits? Celebrations are among the most significant ways we have to proclaim our respect and gratitude, to renew our sense of community, and to remind ourselves of the values and history that bind us together. Ceremonies and rituals create community, binding individuals to the corporate spirit.

Employee engagement and satisfaction improve when leaders bring people together to rejoice in their achievements and to reinforce their shared principles by celebrating values and victories. By bringing people together, sharing lessons from success, and becoming personally involved, leaders reinforce in others the courage required to get extraordinary things done. To Encourage the Heart the leader must recognize contributions to projects as well as to the day-to-day activities; reinforce individuals as well as teams; build informal social support among team members; and celebrate accomplishments—both large and small. Leaders who effectively Celebrate Values and Victories master two essentials:

* Create a spirit of community
* Be personally involved

Create a spirit of community. Leaders who wish to create a spirit of community should ensure that what leaders preach and what leaders celebrate are one and the same. If they aren't, the event will be seen as insincere and phony and leaders' credibility will suffer. Instead leaders should ensure the authenticity of connecting celebration, community, and commitment. Leaders celebrate accomplishments in public to add significant and lasting contributions to individuals and to the organization. Public events can showcase examples of what the organization stands for. Leaders can showcase role models, reminding everyone of why people are there and of the values and visions that they share. Leaders must consider how to make celebrations a part of organizational life, ensuring that they serve a dual purpose: to honor a principle or an achievement and to create community. Ceremonies and celebrations provide social support and are opportunities to build healthier groups. Leaders use celebrations to build supportive relationships, which are important to maintain personal and organizational vitality. Finally, leaders create a spirit of community by having fun. Leaders set the tone to ensure that work does not become all drudgery.

Be personally involved. Leadership is a relationship, and people are much more likely to enlist in initiatives led by those with whom they feel a personal attachment. This human connection between leaders and constituents ensures more commitment and more support. Celebration and community only work when they're genuine. Leaders must be genuine to be truly involved. Leaders set the example that communicates how the organization will celebrate values and victories. Leaders do this by showing that they care by being accessible and in touch with constituents. This happens when they visit workplaces, meet customers, tour plants, recruit at universities, eat with employees, listen to complaints, go to celebrations, and tell stories of success. This makes leaders more genuine and approachable. Exemplary leaders are out and about all the time. Leaders can also be personally involved by perpetuating stories. Stories are helpful in providing inspiration to individuals facing challenging situations and for passing along lessons that people learn.

Encourage the Heart cannot be left to happenstance. Leaders know that recognition and celebration, when done with authenticity and from the heart, build a strong sense of collective identify and community spirit that can carry a group through extraordinarily difficult times. To summarize, Encourage the Heart focuses on two commitments.

- **Commitment 9:** Recognize contributions by showing appreciation for individual excellence.
- **Commitment 10:** Celebrate the values and victories by creating a spirit of community.

Leaders get the best from others not by building fires under people, but by building the fire within them. Leaders who give away their praise reap unexpected dividends.

ENCOURAGE THE HEART: PRACTICE FOR THE LPI ITEMS

The following six statements refer to the items in the *LPI: Leadership Practices Inventory* that relate to Encourage the Heart. The numbers reference the item number in the LPI. These items are numbered and listed in the order as they appear in the LPI. This is done to make it easy to locate each item in this book; the order in which the items are discussed in this book does not suggest an order of importance. You need to determine, based on your client's feedback, which items your client wants to work on and in what sequence.

After each item, you will find suggested questions and activities. These are created for a coaching situation and may be used with the leader(s) you may be coaching. Several of the activities reference a "journal." There is an assumption that your leader will have a personal journal in which to track plans, questions, and desires. A journal is an important tool for reflection on a leader's journey to excellence.

Note: There are many more activities than you would ever use with one person. Work with your client to identify one that will be most useful. Even better, have your clients create their own after you present some possibilities. Remember, the value of these activities and discussion questions is not in the doing, but in the follow-on discussion with you, the coach. Be sure to allow time to discuss the "so what" and the "now what" that occur as a result of any discussion or activity.

At the end of this chapter you will find a resource list that includes books, articles, websites, and blogs for you or your client to use. You will also find a section titled "How the Coach Models This Practice," which serves as a reminder to you about what you must do to be a positive, proactive model for your client.

5. I praise people for a job well done.

Questions You Can Ask

- How do you define praise?
- How do you define a "job well done"?
- What standards define a "job well done"? How are you measuring them?
- What shared values guide decisions people should be making and actions they should be taking?
- What kind of praise do you prefer? What is rewarding for you?
- What kind of praise does each of your team members prefer?
- What opportunities do you have to observe praiseworthy events?
- How can you ensure that you have opportunities to praise people for doing a good job?

- On what occasions, for example, group meetings, one-on-ones, walking the halls, do you praise people? What occasions could you add to your list?
- What does praise look like to you?
- How can I best support you to be able to conduct more praise for a job well done?

Activities You Can Suggest

- **Improve How You Encourage the Heart:** Meet with several co-workers. Hand each of them several index cards. Ask them to write down one idea per card for what you need to change in order to be more positive, energetic, motivating, and inspiring—just one per card. While the individuals are doing this, busy yourself with something else so they do not feel rushed. Gather the cards, shuffle them, and deal them out. Deal some to yourself, too. Go around the table and have each person read one. Don't disagree with the recommended improvement. Thank the person for the idea and move on to the next one. Collect the cards and deal them out again, this time just to your co-workers. Ask them each to read the suggested improvement and on the other side of the index card to provide you with some ideas for how to make the change. This time have them read their own cards. Thank them profusely for spending time with you and for their great suggestions. Sort the cards into categories that you could work on at the same time. Prioritize the stacks. Grab the top priority and get to work.
- **Your Take:** Take a piece of paper and draw a T-grid. At the top of one side place a plus (+) sign; at the top of the other side place a minus (−) sign. List all the positive aspects of recognition under the plus sign. List all the drawbacks of recognition under the minus sign. Share your thoughts with your coach to explore your beliefs about recognition.
- **What's Important:** The most powerful motivator for employees is personalized, instant recognition from their managers. Over and over, five motivating techniques top the list. They include:
  - Personal congratulations from a supervisor.
  - A personal note about good performance from a supervisor.
  - Promotions based on performance.
  - Public recognition for good performance.
  - Meetings to celebrate successes.
  Try at least one of these within the next week.

- *One Minute Manager:* Let's remember *The One Minute Manager* and Ken Blanchard's advice to us:
  - Praise people immediately.
  - Be specific when you tell them what they did right.
  - Tell people how good you feel about what they did right and how it helps the organization.
  - Encourage them to do more of the same.

  Use these *One Minute Manager* ideas as a guide when recognizing others. Make sure the recognition immediately follows the action, that your positive feedback is specific, and that you disclose how good it makes you feel. Think of creative ways to reward others for the work they do. Track yourself on this advice. What did you do well? What could you improve?

- **Listen for Ideas:** A recognized quote by activist author Jack Nichols states, "Every person I work with knows something better than me. My job is to listen long enough to find it and use it." How does this quote pertain to your ability to reward your department? How can you implement this concept in your daily work?

- **One New Thing:** Learn one new thing that is important to every team member on your staff. Then find ways to keep the discussion alive with them, making comments or asking questions. Knowing that you care about them personally is important, and it provides you with more opportunities to add praise.

- **Power of Praise:** Find ways to praise your direct reports, co-workers, peers, even your boss! Here are a few ideas to consider:
  - Invite a team member to breakfast or lunch and ask what matters most to him or her and what you can do as a leader to support that future dream.
  - Send a personal hand-written note thanking someone for something he or she did.
  - Create a funny award to give to individuals for something they've done, such as a hard-boiled egg for "the good egg award" for dealing with a particularly trying customer or a lemon for the "when life gives you lemons, make lemonade" award for dealing positively with a difficult situation.
  - Celebrate an unusual occasion such as Grandparents' Day or Independence Day in another country. Even more unusual—National Garage Sale Day (August 12) or Dick Clark's birthday (November 30). How about food-related celebrations such as Bubble Gum Day (February 1), World Licorice

Day (April 12), Blueberry Month (July), or Waffle Week (the first week in September). Want more suggestions? *The Chase Calendar of Events,* published every year by McGraw-Hill, compiles the most comprehensive list of events. You may wish to do some of these with a peer or ask your team members to plan an event.

10. I make a point to let people know about my confidence in their abilities.

Questions You Can Ask

- What determines capability?
- How confident are you that each of your team members is capable of achieving what is needed for the team? What do you do to address those members you doubt are capable?
- What relationship (if any) do you see between confidence and reinforcement/recognition? Confidence and capability?
- What do you use to measure your "confidence in their abilities"?
- What do you suppose occurs when you doubt anyone's ability?
- Imagine that everyone on your team is 100 percent capable of achieving what he or she must. What would have to happen for the team to reach that place?
- How does showing confidence in others' abilities advance your organization's goals?

Activities You Can Suggest

- **First Impressions:** There is never a second chance for a first impression. Go to www.mindtools.com/CommSkll/FirstImpressions.htm. Read through the information. Identify the things that could help you make a good first impression. Take what you read a step further. What else can you do that will help you to be more positive? Energetic? Motivating? Inspiring? Capture your ideas in a journal and begin to practice immediately. Communication is something that you do every day, so you have many opportunities to practice.
- **Dale Carnegie:** Dale Carnegie's book, *How to Win Friends and Influence People,* is considered one of the most influential books of the 20th century. Many people have followed his principles to become success stories in their own right. Go

to www.dalecarnegie.com to learn more about these principles, to help you see how you can show your confidence in others. You may also want to sign up for an email of free weekly success tips or consider taking a Dale Carnegie course locally.

- **Other Focused:** Observe your interactions with others over the next week—both at work and at home. Note the amount of time that your interchange is focused on others and how much is focused on you. Find ways to tip the scale in their favor if it isn't already.

- **High Expectations:** Napoleon described leaders as "dealers in hope." Have confidence in others' abilities and they will rarely let you down. The key is to be yourself—the more positive side of you! Begin to live life from that side every day so that you don't even need to think about it any more. Love life. Be passionate about what you do. Think positively. Say something nice. Give people hope. Find the best in every situation. Share yourself. The world is full of givers and takers. Be a giver; share your wisdom, your courage, your support. It will come back to you. List five specific things in your journal that you can do that will build confidence for five different individuals on your team.

- **Notable Quotables:** Start a notebook of quotes (or a quote section in your journal) that inspire you. They may be quotes you jot down from an article or book you read; they may be words spoken by someone on the radio; they may be quotes from some of your favorite heroes and speakers, such as Abraham Lincoln or Martin Luther King, Jr.; they may come from actors or actresses; they may be cartoons you rip out of the Sunday comics section; they may be something your grandmother always said; they may be ads with catch phrases; or they may be phrases that you say. Whatever they are and wherever they come from, begin your quote notes today. Continue to add to them. Review them. Re-read them. If they inspired you once, they will again. And if they inspire you, they will inspire someone else. Share them to show confidence in others.

- **First Impressions Game:** Try this the next time you attend a social event. Use John Maxwell's concept (from *The 21 Indispensable Qualities of a Leader*) and put a "10" on everyone you meet's head. How do you do that? Expect the best of them. Expect that each will be the most interesting person you meet all night. Learn and use names. Be positive. Be curious. Focus on others' interests. Finally, be sure to treat everyone as a "10." You will be known as the best party attendee—not that that is your goal. Your goal is to practice making everyone feel like the most important person at the social event. Now

113

take your newfound skill back to the workplace. Put a confidence level of "10" on everyone's head. What do you notice?

- **Post an Idea:** Hang a poster board on the wall and invite team members to submit ideas on a variety of topics. For example, one week you could ask for ideas about how to enhance efficiency, another week you could ask for ideas about how to improve the supply room, and another week you could ask for ideas about how to improve the customers' experience. This is not about solving problems, but about being confident that they have good ideas. Your confidence in them will raise their confidence in themselves.

- **Past Bosses:** List all your recent bosses on a piece of paper. School teachers, professors, or coaches will work as well. Next to their names rate the level of caring and/or interest you believe each showed in you as high, medium, or low. Identify how each behaved. What did he or she do or say that made you rate him or her the way you did? Compare these behaviors and statements with what you do. What can you glean from these ideas that you can implement?

15. I make sure that people are creatively recognized for their contributions to the success of our projects.

Questions You Can Ask

- Let's examine this statement and define each word. What do these words mean to you: People (who are they)? Creatively? Recognized? Contributions? Success? Our projects? And when you put them all together again, what does this mean?
- Why is "creatively" important?
- Why do you think it is important to recognize people for their contributions?
- What kinds of creative recognitions have you provided recently?
- How much peer-to-peer recognition do you see? Why do you suppose that is?
- What two steps could you take immediately that would make the greatest difference?

Activities You Can Suggest
Use ideas from the Recognition Encyclopedia below.

114

RECOGNITION ENCYCLOPEDIA*

Recognition for a job well done is a top motivator for employee performance. Many managers immediately translate this to forms of recognition that increase employees' paychecks—raises and promotions. Yet employees are more often motivated by personal, thoughtful recognition that shows true appreciation for a job well done.

There are many creative things you can do to recognize employees in creative, personalized ways. The following informal incentives provide dozens of ideas for recognizing employees—those you supervise, as well as co-workers who are your colleagues. The list of ideas will get you started, but will also help you begin to think creatively of your own personal ideas.

Personalized Notes

Have a stack of congratulations and thank-you cards ready to add your personal note.

Write notes on personalized note cards.

Create your own note cards:

- Above and beyond
- Thanks a bunch (flowers)
- Good on ya! (or whatever phrase of encouragement you use)
- GRRRREAT job (tiger)
- Bravo
- Or whatever your personal saying of appreciation happens to be

Trophies

Trophies can be one-time items, light-hearted in nature, or they may be more serious. You may also have traveling trophies that move from employee to employee that are kept on permanent display.

(Continued)

One-Time Trophies

- Top banana award (a real banana)
- Lemonade award (lemon for turning lemons into lemonade)
- High-flying award (a glider or kite with a personalized note written on it)
- Donut award (Texas-sized donut to portray, "do not" give up)
- "Atta boy" and "Atta girl" printed note pads
- Blue ribbon awards (purchase at card store or make your own)

Permanent One-Time Trophies

- Plaques for special achievements are always welcome, especially if they are personalized
- MVP award accompanied by a ball cap with a logo

Permanent Traveling Trophies and Awards

- Chalk one up for _____ (chalkboard hanging in a prominent place)
- Top dog (stuffed toy dog that moves from team member to team member)
- Name a conference room, hallway, or display case after a team member for a time period

Thank You Things

Dollar-store type items can be kept in your drawer for a new kind of on-the-spot thank you. Create a story the first time you give the item away to personalize the award for your team members:

- Compass (you found your way through it)
- Bubble gum or glue (you stuck to it)
- Crayons (coloring out of the lines, creative idea, or out-of-the-box thinking)
- LifeSavers® (you saved the day)
- Stars—brass, glow in the dark, etc. (all-star award)
- Gold paperclips (you're golden)
- Plastic apple (teaching someone something difficult)

- Feathers (a feather in your cap for ____)
- Horns (you should be tooting your horn)
- Tape measure (you more than measure up)
- Golf or tennis balls (you're really on the ball)
- Kite (you're flying high)
- Light bulb (bright idea)

Give Your Time

Managers can give their time in many ways, such as:

- Helping out during stressful times
- Offering to do the least-liked task for a day, a week
- Washing the team member's car during break
- Taking the time to use team members' names

Food

Food is always welcomed and can be used and delivered in many ways:

- Bring a brown-bag lunch for the team member
- Provide any snack item
- Arrange to give out "coffee tokens" from a local coffee shop

Surprises

Everyone loves a surprise, and this is a way to add fun to work, too:

- A flower or bouquet from the manager's garden
- Blow up a picture of the person to poster size, posted with a personal note
- Have a cartoon drawn of the team member (talented people can be found in every organization)
- Use large chart paper and hand-make a giant thank-you or congratulations card
- Balloon bouquet
- Toy or book for the team member's child
- Purchase something for the team member's hobby

(Continued)

- Take candid pictures of team members; when the time comes you'll have them ready to enlarge or turn into a collage or card
- Have someone outside the team bestow an award

Department or Group Awards

Awards can be given to the entire department to celebrate specific accomplishments or difficult assignments:

- Managers do the cooking and serving at a cookout
- Bring donuts or fruit
- Bring a cake or cookies baked by the manager
- Schedule monthly cake and coffee with the boss when everyone can discuss how it's going
- Have ongoing metric display of how well we are doing on a special project
- Bell ringer: for special occasions when something extraordinary happens, the manager walks through area ringing a bell
- Have a breakfast meeting off site; manager makes the pancakes
- Recognize efforts during weekly staff meetings
- Sponsor a party
- Sponsor a stress relief day: bring in a speaker, hire someone to give shoulder rubs; the price of admission is to tell one good, politically correct joke and post a cartoon on the bulletin board

Learning as a Reward

Learning new things can be one of the most rewarding things for many employees:

- Attend a tradeshow
- Attend a conference
- Visit a customer
- Benchmark another organization for ideas
- Pay dues so that employees can join professional organizations
- Attend a class
- Attend a workshop
- Professional journal or magazine subscription

- Give the team member a book to help him or her learn something new
- Give a book and have it inscribed by one of the key leaders

Work as a Reward

Work as a reward? Yes, one of the reasons people appreciate their jobs the most is due to meaningful work when employees are

- Allowed to select projects
- Given special, meaningful assignments
- Assigned to a high-profile team or section
- Allowed to work with management on a project
- Named on a project or report that goes up the chain
- Attend a top-level meeting with the manager
- Assigned to a forum of top employees (could be across departments) who meet regularly to discuss issues of interest to them (cater lunch or serve beverages and cookies)
- Named "boss for the day"
- Given an investment of budget for a good idea
- Given personal development time on the job, such as reading
- Provided more autonomy

*The Recognition Encyclopedia is copyrighted by ebb associates inc, Norfolk, VA. Permission granted for use.

20. I publicly recognize people who exemplify commitment to shared values.

Questions You Can Ask

- How do you publicly recognize people?
- What kinds of shared values do you recognize and reward? Can you give a few examples?
- What kind of a role model do you think you are for recognizing others? What would make you better?
- How often do you relate recognition stories of your teammates in front of others? Do you think this is often enough?

- What would it take to reach each team member's capacity for having enough recognition?
- What would you be trying to achieve by giving more/better public recognition of shared values?
- How important do you think this is to your team? To teamwork?

Activities You Can Suggest

- **Appreciation Quote:** "Brains, like hearts, go where they are appreciated." What does this quote by Robert McNamara mean to you? How do you translate this quote into something beneficial to the organization? What does this tell you to do?
- **Catch 'em Exemplifying a Value:** When you see an employee acting out a shared value, compliment the person on the spot. Add why the value is important to the team.
- **Tell Stories:** Share what your employees have done with other department leaders. Word will get around that you've been out on the praise trail again. Tell these same stories at home to your family. Your job will come alive for them.
- **Recognition—Pass It On:** Find a quiet place and think of times when you felt most valued by the organization.
  - What was the situation?
  - What did others do to create the climate in which you felt valued?
  - What did your supervisor do?
  - What contributions did you make, and how were you recognized for these contributions?
  - How would you describe the impact?
  Pause and think about your responses. Now think about today.
  - What contributions are your fellow team members currently making?
  - What would you lose if they were not present?
  - How often do you tell them you appreciate their contributions?
  - How often do you recognize their progress?
  List all the people for whom you have been somewhat negligent in recognizing their progress, contributions, and achievements. Think about how you are going to rectify this. Begin now.
- **Peer-to-Peer Recognition:** As the manager, you cannot be everywhere all the time. Make it easy for all of your staff to reward each other. Let them know you expect it.

- Have organization thank-you notes printed that everyone can use.
- Post a bulletin board where team members can thank other team members, post congratulations to each other, or simply say nice things about each other.
- Recognize and thank people who recognize others.
- Repeat positive remarks that you hear about team members from others.
- "I caught you doing something good" card (could be permanent or passed on).
- **Formal Public Recognition:** Find more formal public opportunities to gain recognition for your team members, such as:
  - Nominate team members for organizational awards.
  - Publish an article in the organization's newsletter about the team member's success.
  - Write a letter of praise recognizing the specific contributions and send a copy to your boss.
  - Add a letter about special achievements to an employee's employment file.
- **Thank You:** Remember to say thank you in the moment and in public. Recognition doesn't need a special time.
- **Invite the Family:** If one of your team members is receiving an award or being recognized by you or the organization, invite his or her family to participate in the ceremony. Have a plan before they arrive. Who will greet them? Where can they await the ceremony? How can you make them feel welcome and comfortable?
- **Publish Awards:** Be sure to contact your internal communication department when you are recognizing people in your department. They can send an email blast or publish the individual's story and picture in a company newsletter.
- **Organization Award:** Use the ideas in the Recognition Encyclopedia to develop an award for your organization. In order to be special and worthwhile, it should address the biggest concern that the organization has. Work with your supervisor to do this. You may choose to have a traveling trophy. It is often not the value of the award, but that individuals are recognized for their contributions.
- **Reward Me; Reward You:** What is rewarding for one person may not be rewarding for another. List all of your direct reports. Next identify what you believe is most rewarding for each person when he or she is successful. Consider these:
  - Does he like a challenge?
  - Is she a check-off-the-list person, liking the accomplishment itself?
  - Does he want public or personal praise?

- Does she want something tangible, such as a certificate?
- Does he want to be asked for insight or ideas or opinions?
- Does she like to learn new things?
- Does he like being in the "in the know"?
- Does she like autonomy, to make her own decisions?
- Does he want a chance at promotions?

Review your list with your supervisor or coach. Does he or she agree with you? What suggestions does your coach or supervisor have that would be motivating as well as equitable for recognizing the progress and achievement of each person?

25. I tell stories of encouragement about the good works of others.

Questions You Can Ask

- How do you define a good story?
- How can a story be encouraging?
- How often does a member of your team do something worth telling others about? Do you know about the good works of team members that occur outside the business?
- What kind of stories would you like to be told about you?
- How could you redefine storytelling so that it could occur more often?
- What are you going to do to improve this behavior?
- Think back to the most recognize and praise worthy time in your career. What was happening and how could you convey an encouraging story to someone about this time?
- What kind of game plan do you need to move forward on this?

Activities You Can Suggest

- **What You Don't Know:** Learn about each other. Use a warm-up activity at your next staff meeting. Ask the question, "What is one thing that people in the room would not know about you?" You should be prepared with a couple of things about yourself as examples. You might say things such as, "Few people would imagine that I love to drive on icy roads" or "Few people would imagine that I won the spelling bee in my school when I was in eighth grade" or "Few people would imagine that

I like to write poetry in my spare time." This activity helps to show that you have a personal interest in the interests of your team members. More importantly, it models how each of them can also express an interest in his or her co-workers.

- **It's Not Over:** You don't need to wait until a project is over before you recognize each team member's successful milestones. Your team will appreciate a pizza brought in when they are in the middle of a project that is keeping them past normal working hours. Share in each other's milestones!

- **Department Share Day:** Set at least one day each year aside for a department picnic or party that celebrates the entire team and shares the contributions they have made.

- **I Felt Valued:** Meet with a co-worker who is in a similar position to yours from another department. Each of you should think of times when you felt most valued by the organization and individually answer the following questions on paper:
  - What was the situation?
  - What did others do to create the climate where you felt valued?
  - What did your supervisor do?
  - What contributions did you make and how were you recognized for these contributions?
  - How was your contribution celebrated?
  - How would you describe the impact?

  Pause and discuss your responses. Listen to each other's situations. Now discuss the following questions:
  - What contributions are your fellow team members currently making?
  - What would you lose if they were not present?
  - How often do you tell them you appreciate their contributions?
  - What will each of you do as a result of this exercise?

- **What Does This Skill Mean?** Meet with your supervisor/coach to more clearly define what this skill truly means and how it relates to the vision of the organization. During your conversations try to narrow down "what" this skill means. Ask him or her to talk to you about what he or she does. Ask the person to observe you over the next week or two to gather specific examples that he or she can share with you. Put the suggestions into practice immediately.

- **Invite Ideas:** Ask your team members to create a list of creative ways to tell stories of encouragement. Use this list frequently, and, by the way, share the story about the completion of the list with the entire team!

- **Learn How to Motivate:** Take a class or attend a conference that addresses motivating team members. You will find that there is no one way to motivate. You truly must identify what is important to each person. Focus on celebrations and how each person defines celebration. Expand your definition of celebration. What does a celebration mean to each of your team members?
- **Local Celebration:** Attend a celebration outside of work. It could be a block party, a children's birthday party, a church chili supper, or another. Identify the aspects that made it worth sharing. How could you use these same aspects to share the accomplishments of your team members?
- **Motivational Tools:** Use your search engine to identify reward and recognition tools. The 7,220,000 sites that came up as of this writing should provide you with at least a couple of ideas to add to your toolbox! Give yourself a deadline to implement at least three by Thursday.

30. I get personally involved in recognizing people and celebrating accomplishments.

Questions You Can Ask

- How do you define recognizing people? How do you define celebrating accomplishments? If you are better at one or the other, which one?
- What examples can you think of when you received recognition for your contribution? What effect did it have on you?
- If you tracked the number of times you provide recognition to team members as individuals and as a group, what do you think it would show?
- Why is showing recognition important to a team?
- When is it the most difficult for you to show recognition and celebrate accomplishments for your team?
- What could you do to increase the amount of recognition you show?
- What obstacles prevent you from giving lots of recognition or celebrating accomplishments?
- What are some ideas you have to celebrate the accomplishments of others?

Activities You Can Suggest

- **Celebrate Success:** For big successes, such as reaching a milestone, completing a successful project, and so forth, find ways to celebrate the team's success that recognize going the extra mile: time off, take them to lunch, a bouquet of balloons to greet them at the end of the project. Challenge yourself to implement something you have never done to show appreciation to one of your teams immediately.

- **Tap the Team:** Before beginning a project, ask the team members what would be rewarding for them. Keep that in mind as the project winds down. Then implement what they told you was rewarding.
- **Team Tribute:** When you have a team that is working on a highly visible project or is under a short timeline, try to find a unique way to celebrate the accomplishment. One thing you could do for a special project is to invite the CEO or some other high-level leader to come to your department to congratulate him or her.
- **Party Hearty:** Visit your local party store. Purchase a few themed items (napkins, cups, banners, candles) so that you will always be ready for a spontaneous celebration. All you'll need to do is add the refreshments.
- **Team Appreciation Project:** Circulate an email to your colleagues in other departments putting out a call for their ideas about how they recognize teams. You could perhaps compile all the ideas and email them back to everyone who contributed.
- **Pat on the Back:** Be aware of the recognition (or lack thereof) that you give your spouse and children at home. You could use some of the ideas from the Recognition Encyclopedia at home and stir up lots of excitement. Try to use something different every time.
- **Special Day:** Invent a reason to show recognition. Invent and sponsor a special day, perhaps a special dress day, for example, Hawaiian day or jeans day, or favorite team day to celebrate the end of a difficult project or an especially difficult day at work.
- ***Encouraging the Heart***: Read the book, *Encouraging the Heart*. Don't have time for the entire book? Turn to page 151 to read 151 ideas for Encouraging the Heart. The ideas will make you think of more of your own.

BOOKS, ARTICLES, AND WEBSITES

Books for Encourage the Heart

- Richard Boyatzis and Annie McKee. *Resonant Leadership*. Boston: Harvard Business School Press, 2005.
- Nathen Branden. *The Six Pillars of Self-Esteem*. New York: Bantam Books, 1994.
- Ken Blanchard and Sheldon Bowles. *Gung Ho! Turn on the People in Any Organization*. New York: William Morrow, 1997.

- John Hope Bryant. *Love Leadership: The New Way to Lead in a Fear-Based World*. San Francisco: Jossey-Bass, 2009.
- Terrence Deal and M. K. Deal. *Corporate Celebrations: Play, Purpose, and Profit at Work*. San Francisco: Berrett-Koehler, 1998.
- Dave Hemsath and Leslie Yerkes. *301 Ways to Have Fun at Work*. San Francisco: Berrett-Koehler, 1997.
- James M. Kouzes and Barry Z. Posner. *Encouraging the Heart: A Leader's Guide to Rewarding and Recognizing Others*. San Francisco: Jossey-Bass, 1999.
- Ellen J. Langer. *Mindfulness*. Reading, MA: Addison-Wesley, 1989.
- Bob Nelson. *1001 Ways to Reward Employees*. New York: Workman, 1994.
- Tom Rath and Donald Clifton. *How Full Is Your Bucket: Positive Strategies for Work and Life*. New York: Gallup Press, 2004.

Articles

- "How to Pitch a Brilliant Idea," *Harvard Business Review,* September 2003. Before you even know it, the stranger across the desk has decided what kind of person you are. Knowing how you'll be stereotyped allows you to play to—and control—the other guy's expectations.
- "Leadership and the Small Group," *T+D,* July 2008. Peter Block explains why it is important that leaders know how to convene small groups, ask questions, and listen.
- "Discovering Your Authentic Leadership," *Harvard Business Review,* February 2007. We all have the capacity to inspire and empower others. But we must first be willing to devote ourselves to our personal growth and development as leaders.
- "Communicate to Inform, Not Impress," *Harvard Business Review,* February 2006. It's all too easy to fall into the trap of using the important-sounding but vague expressions that constitute so much business communication today. But jargon is bad news—not because it irritates English teachers and editors, but because it will bore, confuse, and alienate your audience. Read this article to learn how to break free of the tedium, obscurity, and anonymity traps of business language to become a more informative, interesting, and persuasive communicator.
- "Taking the Talent Pulse: What Drives High Potentials?" *Talent Management,* May 2008. An organization's high-potential talent often is courted for its ability to contribute a disproportionate amount of the company's success. Discusses what keeps these valued employees motivated and passionate.

Websites/Blogs

- www.baudville.com. Billed as "the place for daily recognition," this website is full of awards, do-dads, and complete systems to help you recognize employees.
- www.dalecarnegie.com for information about the concepts that have been successful since 1912 and the training that evolved from the belief in the power of self-improvement. Training sharpens skills to improve performance in order to build positive, steady, and profitable results.
- www.evite.com. A website that can help you plan the logistics of an entire event to celebrate your followers or one in particular.
- www.hallmark.com. For access to eCards you can send to your constituents.

HOW THE COACH MODELS THIS PRACTICE

- Praise the leader for a job well done—often.
- Make a point of letting the leader know that you have faith and confidence in his or her ability to be an exemplary leader. Use examples of ways in which he or she has already done a good job.
- Find creative ways to reward the leader for accomplishments, both large and small. Identify what the leader finds rewarding and vary the rewards, perhaps a handwritten note, a relevant cartoon you've cut out of a magazine, a book that is pertinent to the leader, something related to his or her hobby, something you have discussed as an aside, such as a favorite recipe, or other things that would have personal appeal.
- Publicly recognize the leader as appropriate. For example, if you run into his or her supervisor in the hall, a quick comment about positive progress may be appropriate.
- When a leader achieves a particularly difficult milestone, celebrate the accomplishments with refreshments from the local coffee shop or homemade cookies you baked.
- Provide appreciation and support for your leader's hard work, always being on time, or other things that are meaningful.

PART II
IMPROVE YOUR COACHING COMPETENCE

CHAPTER 7: COACHING FOR SUCCESS

In This Chapter

- Explore the recent history of coaching.
- Consider the definition of coaching.
- Review the benefits of coaching.
- Explore the challenges of coaching.
- Reflect on whether you have the temperament to be a coach.
- Present various roles that coaches play.

You are probably familiar with corporate interest in coaching and have picked up this book because you want to learn more. Perhaps you are considering coaching or you already are a coach and you want to brush up on your skills. Perhaps you are a seasoned coach and are looking for a few additional tips. Or perhaps you have picked up this book because you have completed a great deal of work with *The Leadership Challenge* materials in the past and this book provides you with another way to dig deeper into the content.

This chapter, the first in Part II, provides you with a brief history of coaching. It also reviews some of the benefits of coaching for everyone who is involved. If you have never been involved in coaching, it will introduce several ideas for you to ponder, including whether you have the temperament to be a coach.

A BRIEF AND RECENT HISTORY OF COACHING

Coaching has been around for a long time—perhaps from the earliest human interaction as the more experienced and skilled taught those who were less experienced how to cook, hunt, communicate with cave-wall graphics, build a fire, and other techniques of survival.

History tells us that the French statesman Cardinal Richelieu (1585–1642) relied on advice from Father Francois Leclerc du Tremblay. As head of the Royal Council and prime minister of France, Richelieu made clever decisions for King Louis XIII.

Current coaching has its roots in sports to some extent, beginning with Timothy Gallway's *The Inner Game of Tennis*, published in 1974. This book dismissed some of the behaviorism psychology prevalent at the time and shifted the focus of performance from physical action to a mental mindset. The popularity of the book spread, and coaching became a buzzword in the 1980s in many corporate settings. Books, articles, and dissertations attempted to define and promote coaching. The Coaches Training Institute, The Worldwide Association of Business Coaches, and the International Coach Federation were established to train coaches and ensure the integrity of the practice.

One of the first and most influential models for coaching is GROW (goal, reality, options, will) published in *Coaching for Performance*, by Sir John Whitmore in 1992. Anthony Robbins' and Stephen Covey's books and workshops fueled the desire for personal development through coaching. Coaching became more common as corporations recognized that a more individualized approach to executive learning was a better investment for both the individual and the organization.

Currently, a majority of Fortune 500 companies hire coaches to work with upper management. Coaching continues to grow and change. Just a little more than a decade ago, coaching was seen as "punishment" for leaders who needed to improve specific areas. Today, coaching is seen as a valuable perk for even the best leaders in an organization.

WHAT IS COACHING?

With the field in flux and growing rapidly, you can imagine that there are many definitions of coaching. Here are a few we found when doing our research.

"An interactive process to help individuals and organizations develop more rapidly and produce more satisfying results; improving others' ability to set goals, take action, make better decisions, and make full use of their natural strengths."

International Coach Federation website
(www.internationalcoachfederation.org)

Coaching for Success

*"Coaching is a meaningful, accountable relationship
created by having routine one-on-one conversations
about the coachee's full experience and power of possibility."*

Oberstein, *10 Steps to Successful Coaching*,
2009, p. 10.

*". . . commitment to align beliefs with actions. Coaching
leaders communicate powerfully, help others to create
desired outcomes, and hold relationships based on
honesty, acceptance, and accountability."*

Bianco-Mathis, Nabors, and Roman,
*Leading from the Inside Out:
A Coaching Model,* 2002, p. 4.

*". . . challenging and supporting people in
achieving higher levels of performance while allowing
them to bring out the best in themselves and
those around them."*

Hargrove, *Masterful Coaching*, 1995, p. 15.

*"Professional coaching is an ongoing relationship
which focuses on the client taking action toward the
realization of their vision, goal, or desires."*

Professional and Personal Coaching Association

As you can see, there is no shortage of definitions. As you read more about coaching, you will find that some of the definitions, descriptions, and philosophies even contradict one another. Therefore, it may be beneficial for you to begin to formulate your own definition. What do you believe coaching is about, especially as it relates to *The Leadership Challenge* materials and the *Leadership Practices Inventory* (LPI)?

133

WHY COACHING?

An organization's success depends on its talent—its ability to maximize its talent and to retain it. To be successful, an organization needs to enable its workforce to grow, develop, and mature. Coaching is one way to support continued employee development and can be a powerful tool for improving the performance of both the individual and the organization. Coaching can help retain high performers, improve job performance, reduce learning time, support knowledge sharing, and promote individual development.

Coaching can address both personal and professional skill development that is not possible in any type of classroom or e-learning setting. In addition to providing opportunities to acquire valuable skills and knowledge, coaching involves the opportunity for individuals to set stretch goals and receive one-on-one guidance. A good coaching program provides a risk-free environment in which individuals can learn valued skills that help them reach their full potential.

All of these are true as you consider using a coaching model to help leaders to better implement The Five Practices of Exemplary Leadership®. Specifically, coaching for The Five Practices can:

- Help leaders focus on developing precise critical skills within The Five Practices.
- Develop high-potential leaders to be more effective than they already are.
- Round out leaders' daily behaviors by identifying specific actions they can take to implement The Five Practices.
- Provide a sounding board for leaders who may be uncertain about the exact definition or implementation of The Five Practices.
- Facilitate a transition to another position as a leader moves from a comfortable current job to a new one.
- Address derailing behavior that a leader may not be aware of or understand.

BENEFITS OF COACHING

Coaching benefits the individual and the organization, but have you ever thought about the fact that it benefits you, the coach, as well? Let's explore some of the benefits of coaching in general and, more specifically, coaching for the improved implementation of The Five Practices.

Benefits to the Organization

Coaching leaders may be seen as a costly proposition; however, it also has the following benefits to the organization:

- Promotes organizational consistency when using the common language and focus provided by The Five Practices.
- Furthers leadership development by facilitating the implementation and understanding of leadership skills.
- Reduces turnover as individuals see that the organization wants to invest in them.
- Ensures solid leadership succession by transmitting corporate values and behaviors to the next generation of leaders.
- Improves performance and productivity of both coaches and leaders.
- Improves organizational climate; coaches help leaders understand their impact on others and on organizational success.
- Increases commitment and engagement of high-potential leaders and other employees in general.
- Creates an organization that "talks" about leadership development and actively supports and values learning.
- Creates trust and builds better professional relationships.
- Integrates the corporate strategy and leadership philosophy into individual goals by promoting commitment and engagement.

Benefits to the Individual Leader

Of course, the benefits to leaders are easy to enumerate. After all, the focus is on them and enhancing their leadership capacity. This is something they will have for the rest of their lives and in all situations—not just when interacting within the organization. Some of the benefits include:

- Individualized professional development, especially in the leadership development area.
- Feedback about personal strengths and style.
- Career enhancement and better preparation for other jobs within the organization.
- A better sense of the organization's culture and what it takes to succeed.

- Recipient of the coach's expertise and experience.
- Increased self-awareness and confidence.
- Exploring options and selecting an optimal direction.
- Gain knowledge, skills, and competencies, including approaches and techniques they can use to coach their own employees.
- Enhanced cross-department understanding.

Rewards for You, the Coach

The organization benefits, the individual leaders benefit, so how about you—the coach? Examine these rewards and begin to consider what you find appealing about being a coach. Knowing why you want to coach leaders will help you to get through some of the difficult times of coaching.

- Coaches are viewed by others as contributors to the organization's future.
- Coaches have a chance to make a difference in their organizations.
- By coaching others, coaches review, renew, and upgrade their own professional skills.
- Coaching provides an opportunity to advance one's own career, both internally and externally.
- Coaches contribute to making decisions about things such as the organization's succession planning.
- Organizations respect coaches as developers of leaders.
- Coaches increase their own capacity for leadership.
- Coaches gain intrinsic rewards for contributing to employees and the organization.
- Coaches receive open appreciation for the work they do with leaders.
- Internal coaches gain skills that prepare them to become external coaches in the future.

What motivates you to be a coach? Be clear about your reasons. This will help you to do a better job for your leaders. Coaching is goal-oriented and benefits the organization, the individual leaders, and the coach.

INTERNAL OR EXTERNAL?

Does it make a difference whether you are internal or external to your coaching assignment?

Coaching is a formal arrangement between a coach and a leader. It is generally sponsored by and paid for by an organization. External coaches are generally paid for each meeting or number of hours spent coaching the leaders. Internal coaches, on the other hand, conduct their coaching as a part of their salaried workday. Generally, assignments are limited to key leaders and focus on specific objectives that are important to their career development.

Although the job of the coach is generally the same whether providing services from an internal source, such as the human resources department, or externally from a consulting firm, there are differences you should be aware of. There are advantages and disadvantages for both internal and external coaches. Table 7.1 displays the differences. Whether you are an internal or external coach, you have advantages for approaching the task ahead of you. You also have challenges. Be aware of the challenges—those things that an organization may consider disadvantages. Do what you need to do to overcome the negative perceptions.

How can you overcome some of the disadvantages on the chart?

Both internal and external coaches will be more successful if they use and stick with a specific model. Both will be successful if they are clear about their definition of what coaching is. Both require strong communication and interpersonal skills. Both will be most successful if they have completed some personal work themselves to identify their own strengths and weaknesses. Both will be more successful if they have identified the kinds of questions their clients might ask and what their responses might be to each. Table 7.2 identifies a list of questions that might be asked of a coach from each location, as well as questions that are similar for both.

So whether you work from inside the organization or are hired from the outside, you bring with you a certain set of expectations—some positive, some negative. Investing time and completing your homework is your best preparation for both.

TABLE 7.1. INTERNAL AND EXTERNAL COACHING

Internal Coaches	External Coaches
Advantages	**Advantages**
Better understanding of the organization and its culture	More objective
Better understanding of the leader and the leader's challenges	More experience in different organizations and industries
Less costly	Fresh perspective
More schedule flexibility, allowing more time for observations	Higher credibility
Organization can manage process consistency	Increased confidentiality
Available on short notice	More exposure to a variety of coaching practices As career "professionals," depend on success of every client More likely to have certification
Disadvantages	**Disadvantages**
Perception of less objectivity and confidentiality	Higher cost
Fewer broad coaching experiences	Less knowledgeable of the organization and its culture
Limited exposure to best practices	Increased time to get up-to-speed
Less likely to have certification	Less flexibility in scheduling
Leaders more likely to cancel sessions Leaders may have less respect Leaders may value time less More difficult to challenge upper management May be too close to the situations	Lack of a consistent process with numerous coaches from various organizations

TABLE 7.2. PREPARE FOR THESE QUESTIONS

Internal Coaches

- What experience do you have that ensures you can help me?

- What training or experience have you had that ensures your success?

- What information will you share with my supervisor?
  Your supervisor?

External Coaches

- What is your availability?

- Why do you cost so much?

- What do you know about our organization? How will you get up-to-speed?

- How do I contact you between our scheduled meetings?

Both

- What is coaching?

- How will you guarantee confidentiality?

- What coaching model will you use?

- What will we do? How often will we meet?

- What is your philosophy about coaching?

- What can I expect?

- How do you measure results?

WILL I MAKE A GOOD COACH?

How do you measure up against a list of abilities required to be a coach? In the next chapter, this book takes a more in-depth look at the competencies required to be a coach. You probably have a good idea of your basic temperament to know whether you will be a successful coach. Are you a born coach? Or are you someone who needs to learn and practice the skills to improve your ability to be a coach?

Ask yourself a few questions. What do people say about you? Do they think you are an excellent communicator and even better listener? Do you convey credibility and trustworthiness? Are you objective? Can you give direct, candid feedback? Do you focus on results? Are you adept at asking just the right question that makes people pause? Do you easily build rapport and establish trust? Do people tell you things they may not tell others? Do you have ample business experience? Have you mastered the use of the LPI?

Here's a quick overview. Before you go any further in this book, go through the list and place a check in front of all the items that describe you—those you can respond to with a resounding "YES!" Don't be shy about checking those for which you have achieved excellence. On the other hand, be absolutely honest about those that you still need to improve.

Skills and Competencies

☐ Provides supportive feedback

☐ Identifies creative, practical learning activities

☐ Practices excellent communication and listening skills

☐ Communicates clearly, candidly, and accurately

☐ Is results-oriented

☐ Is a certified coach, or is qualified based on experience and maturity

Characteristics

☐ Motivator and teacher

☐ High performer

☐ Unthreatened by others' success

☐ Challenges others to excellence

☐ Trustworthy and trusting

☐ A people person

☐ Ability to initiate and build a relationship

☐ Upholds and models high ethical standards

☐ Comfortable in a fast-changing environment

☐ Strategic visionary thinker

Attitude and Attributes

☐ Believes in life-long learning

☐ Strongly desires to be a coach

☐ Is competent, confident, and an informal leader

☐ Respected by others

The competencies, characteristics, and attributes above are a brief overview of what's to come. Did you check off all twenty items? Keep any you did not check in mind as we move through the next two chapters of this book. Begin to coach yourself about what it will take for you to get up-to-speed in those areas.

IS YOUR LEADER COACHABLE?

The most successful coaching clients love to learn; they are coachable. They are open to many ideas and new concepts. Other characteristics also help define the ease with which their successes will occur. Characteristics of a successful leader who is open to coaching include some of these.

Self-Understanding

☐ Know themselves well

☐ Know when to ask for help, support, or encouragement

☐ Reflect on situations and relate to themselves

☐ Able to describe their preferred learning styles

☐ Capitalize on their strengths and admit to and work on weaknesses

Good Communicators

☐ Read others well

☐ Listen well

☐ Willing to ask questions

Self-Starters

- ☐ Motivated to try new ideas
- ☐ Act on challenges and recommendations
- ☐ Learn by listening and observing others' successes and failures
- ☐ Set goals and achieve them
- ☐ Identify innovative solutions and don't give up

Appreciate Feedback

- ☐ Willing to discuss problems
- ☐ Value challenges and recommendations
- ☐ Solicit feedback and appreciate it whether correct or not

Self-Assured

- ☐ Willing to be vulnerable in front of those they learn from (mentors, coaches, supervisors)
- ☐ Desire candor and truth
- ☐ Embrace change
- ☐ Are persistent
- ☐ Take risks, challenge themselves, and discover their own resources

Professional

- ☐ Balance personal and professional life
- ☐ Recognize the value of continuous improvement and work at personal growth and learning
- ☐ Admit mistakes and accept them in others
- ☐ Are positive thinkers
- ☐ Balance results and people

Some of your leaders may not be ready for coaching. They may not show up for scheduled meetings with you, may resist feedback you provide, may present many

FIGURE 7.1. THE MANY ROLES OF A COACH

Consultant[1]
Orchestrater
Advisor
Challenger
Helper

---

[1] © 1996 ebb associates inc. Used with permission.

excuses for a lack of accountability, or any number of other things. These concerns are addressed in future chapters.

WHAT DO COACHES DO?

Coaches assume many roles. Figure 7.1 is a depiction of the key roles: consultant, orchestrater, advisor, challenger, and helper. This catch-all list provides a broad picture of how varied a coach's role can be. Let's examine these roles in more detail.

Consultant**

- Creates an environment conducive to personal and professional growth.
- Presents all sides of the leaders' decisions about which gaps to address.
- Focuses on the leader's individual needs, based on the overall needs of the organization.
- Identifies and articulates obstacles that may prevent the leader from being successful.
- Interprets the 360-degree results and provides feedback as it relates to the leader's organizational culture, but not clouded by personal biases or prejudices.
- Provides feedback about how the leader fits into the organization.

Orchestrater

- Expands the leader's network of professional contacts.
- Has access to and recommends a variety of learning opportunities.

** © 1996 ebb associates inc. Used with permission.

- Introduces the leader to new experiences.
- Schedules uninterrupted time with the leader to discuss progress, ideas, setbacks, and next steps.
- Acts as a catalyst to help the leader achieve objectives.

Advisor

- Provides guidance, support, and information and answers questions.
- Provides insight to the organization needs, its culture, and other leaders.
- Suggests developmental needs and recommends appropriate strategies.
- Reviews the leader's development plan, especially as it relates to the feedback from the LPI.
- Offers guidance and insight toward the leader's career plans.
- Acts as a sounding board for ideas and concerns.

Challenger

- Gives honest feedback—candid, constructive, and positive.
- Asks powerful questions to stimulate learning and reflection.
- Encourages the leader to explore new directions or think from a different perspective.
- Challenges the leader to stretch while identifying strategies.
- Questions congruency between the leader's style, values, ideals, and the organization.
- Confronts the leader about a lack of progress.

Helper

- Builds a trusting relationship with the leader.
- Gets to know the leader well.
- Makes time to be available when needed.
- Listens to individual concerns and counsels when possible.
- Guides the leader to resources to assist with problems or concerns.
- Acts as a role model.
- Motivates the leader to continue to achieve high quality success.

MANY ROLES, BUT MOSTLY COACHES COMMUNICATE

Most important overall is the ability of the coach to communicate with the leaders. A coach can accomplish a great deal with good communication. Just how does communication link to these five roles? Here are a few examples.

Consultant

Just as a consultant must convey honest, although sometimes difficult-to-deliver messages, so too must the coach in the consultant role. Feedback provided by a coach needs to be clear, and the process to deliver feedback needs to be candid and straightforward. Coaches must be counted on to tell the truth, no matter how difficult. When providing feedback, a coach focuses on both positive feedback, what the leader is doing well, and constructive feedback, what the leader needs to improve.

In the consultant role, the coach must ensure that sage advice is timely and not provided prematurely. A good consultant obtains all the information before reacting. Plunging in too soon may cut off the data flowing from the leader. Not only might this prevent the coach from hearing vital information, but it may create a barrier that prevents the leader from reaching deep within to access internal thoughts and feelings. This internal reflection process often leads individuals to reach their own solutions. Take care not to stifle this by jumping in with your correct answer.

A coach knows when the time is right to provide information. If not, coaches test the discussion periodically by asking, "Does this make sense?" "Is this helpful?" "What questions do you have at this point?"

Orchestrater

As the name of this role implies, the coach must provide information that brings the leader together with people and experiences to meet the identified goals. The coach initiates the discussion and offers assistance to the leader as needed. The coach may provide a phone number, a name, or an introduction. The coach may also communicate directly with other executives to establish meetings or to introduce the leader to others who can provide assistance.

Coaches may at times conduct some of their own research. They may place a phone call or two around the organization or outside to contacts in search of the right person or event to fulfill a leader's needs. The coach serves as a catalyst and coordinator in this role. The communication skills required may be simply providing information or may also be skills to influence someone else to become involved.

Advisor

As an advisor, the coach will provide suggestions to the leader. However, the coach should not be too hasty and simply "tell" the leader. The basics of good two-way communication should be observed here. While it may take more time to ask open-ended questions or to probe leaders to identify their own solutions, rationale, and insight, it is more beneficial in the long run than merely providing advice.

Leaders may have many questions. Often it may be better if a direct answer is not given. As an advisor, coaches may want to ask questions that will take the leader down the path of self-discovery rather than answering questions or giving information that may close a door to new ideas.

A good advisor ensures that all the facts are out. The coach in the advisor role encourages and values input, opinions, and ideas from the leader and will incorporate them into the leader's growth. This means the coach needs to set aside time to receive input from the leader about people and projects.

Coaches should be certain about the difference between opinion and fact and clearly state which they are providing for the leader. While both are valuable, clarifying which is being stated ensures that the leader knows whether or not the information is based on fact.

Challenger

As the name of this role implies, coaches will want to challenge leaders to stretch, to maximize the time spent during their coaching experience, and to reach their greatest potential. Challenging is the skill of asking the right questions, at the right time, and in the right spirit.

Challenging should not be used to "test" the leader. This may give the impression that the coach is playing a game to prove that the leader does not know something. A coach's challenging role may focus on topics such as:

- Has the leader sufficiently challenged him- or herself with the goals established?
- Is the leader focused on the learning that is occurring? Practicing and internalizing it?
- Is the leader taking every opportunity to implement strategies that have been outlined in the leader's daily work situation?
- Is the leader experimenting with new behaviors? Evaluating the results objectively?
- Is the leader maintaining (or acquiring) a positive attitude?

A coach also offers opposing views. A coach's role is not merely to agree or affirm the leader's beliefs or plans, but to challenge the leader to another way of thinking so all the options are seen. Throughout this discussion the coach maintains a confident and assertive, yet friendly, tone.

A good way to end a challenging discussion is to ask, "What help, advice, information, or direction do you need from me to help you move forward?" This will bring both the coach and the leader back to a less intense discussion than what may take place when the coach is challenging.

Helper

Most often the communication skill required as a helper is to be a good listener. Leaders may face problems and concerns at work or at home. During these times, leaders truly appreciate the trust coaches have built so they can feel comfortable sharing their concerns in a confidential setting. A coach who is patient, empathic listener will not only be appreciated, but will also be a role model for the times when the leaders find themselves in similar situations on the job.

Coaches may ask whether they can help in any way, and generally the response will be "no." Most leaders will not be looking for you to solve their problems, only to share the burden by listening. Having a coach who allows them to talk through issues in a confidential setting is a valuable benefit for leaders.

Motivating a leader to continue to move forward is another imperative communication skill. In the helper role, this may come in many shapes. It may be in the form of inspiration, sharing personal experiences, reinforcement, recognition, or persuasive techniques. Any or all of these may be required to sustain high-quality results.

SUMMARY

A coach who is committed to making the relationship effective will make communication a high priority. A coach's success occurs when communication between the coach and the leader takes the leader from an introduction to The Five Practices through insightful self-critique, to self-motivated learning and wisdom.

The next chapter will provide additional insight to specific competencies required in addition to communication skills.

CHAPTER 8: COACHING COMPETENCIES

In This Chapter

- Evaluate your coaching competencies.
- Review communication skills required by a coach.
- Review interpersonal proficiency required by a coach.
- Review how the ability to build relationships is required by a coach.
- Review ways coaches help clients design developmental plans.
- Review how inspiring action is required by a coach.
- Review how to facilitate the coaching process.

Coaching can be viewed as both an art and a science. This chapter focuses on the competencies a master coach requires, and even though you will read a plethora of skills a coach requires, read between the lines. You will see that a coach not only needs to know what kind of questions to ask, but needs to have a sense about when to use them. A coach not only needs to have a toolbox full of techniques, but must also be perceptive about how to use them. Master coaching requires both the science of tools and techniques and the art of intuition and instinct.

So although coaching is extremely competency-dependent, it also requires maturity and a high level of expertise. If you are a new coach, don't worry; you will build up the experience required to become a wise coach. In the meantime, it is best if you avoid "practicing" with the CEO of your company!

SELF-EVALUATION

Before you continue with this chapter, pause to complete the self-evaluation in Exhibit 8.1. The evaluation provides you with an overview of the many competencies required of a coach. This insight will provide you with direction for your personal improvement. In addition, the results will help you to decide what topics to focus on in this chapter.

EXHIBIT 8.1. ASSESS YOUR COACHING COMPETENCIES*

Use the following scale to rate your coaching skills and knowledge.

1 = No experience or skill
3 = Average skills or knowledge, need to develop this more
5 = Competent, one of my strengths

2 = Minimal ability, definitely need to develop
4 = Above-average ability, doing okay, but could use some shoring up

How do you rate on each of these competencies?

1. ____ Use direct communication
2. ____ Ask powerful questions
3. ____ Use active listening techniques for clear understanding
4. ____ Communicate persuasively using metaphors and analogies
5. ____ Exhibit a variety of response techniques
6. ____ Able to read situations using observations and intuition
7. ____ Aware of and open to the leader's entire situation
8. ____ Present constructive feedback
9. ____ Confront and manage lack of progress
10. ____ Respect everyone from diverse backgrounds
11. ____ Foster collaboration and trust
12. ____ Support and challenge the leader to stay action-oriented
13. ____ Build an intimate rapport and maintain confidentiality
14. ____ Provide recognition that encourages skill building
15. ____ Refrain from giving specific advice
16. ____ Select appropriate data sources and methods
17. ____ Analyze and diagnose needs
18. ____ Generate development options
19. ____ Solve problems
20. ____ Create a results-oriented action plan
21. ____ Recognize a leader's readiness for coaching

22. ____ Encourage a leader's progress toward achieving goals
23. ____ Motivate and inspire leaders to do more than they thought they could
24. ____ Sustain a leader during setbacks
25. ____ Evaluate outcomes
26. ____ Establish a coaching agreement
27. ____ Set measurable objectives
28. ____ Manage time and priorities
29. ____ Monitor and hold leaders accountable to achieve results
30. ____ Link coaching with other organizational learning efforts

* © 2008, 2009 ebb associates inc. Used with permission.

Interpreting Your Scores in Six Skill Clusters

Six critical skill clusters distinguish a successful coach. Although each category holds a cluster of related skills that are distinct from the others, individual skills in each of the clusters are often dependent on individual skills in the other clusters. The questions that pertain to the skill cluster are identified in the parentheses next to each cluster below. For each set of skills, total your scores for those questions and enter your score in the space provided.

Communication Skills (1 to 5)	My score ____
Interpersonal Proficiency (6 to 10)	My score ____
Building Relationships (11 to 15)	My score ____
Designing Developmental Plans (16 to 20)	My score ____
Inspiring Action (21 to 25)	My score ____
Facilitating the Coaching Process (26 to 30)	My score ____

A score of 20 or more in each skill cluster says that you are well on your way to being a master coach. Any questions that you answered with a 2 or lower should give you pause to think about what you can do to improve that particular skill. Any skill clusters with a score of 14 or less should be a signal that you need to focus on improving that set of skills.

Continue Your Personal Evaluation

You may also wish to make several copies of the assessment and ask others you trust to complete the assessment about you, rating your skills. Review the differences between your responses and the responses of others. Look for similar themes. This exercise will provide valuable insight into how others see you.

EXPLORING THE COMPETENCIES

The key competencies discussed in this chapter match those identified in the self-evaluation you just completed. They are presented in the six categories: Communication Skills, Interpersonal Proficiency, Building Relationships, Designing Developmental Plans, Inspiring Action, and Facilitating the Coaching Process. For each category, each item from the self-assessment is explained. Hundreds of ideas are provided for how to build and implement the skills and knowledge required of a coach.

► COMMUNICATION SKILLS

The success of a coaching partnership is steeped in excellent communication. This could relate to a variety of issues such as confidentiality, formality of setting, and body language. Consider these basic communication reminders prior to every coaching meeting.

Appropriate Location. Strike a balance between the various aspects of location. To establish trusting and open communication in your relationship, decide where you will both feel comfortable and free to exchange ideas. Will you both be more comfortable in the leader's office or some other place? The location relates to power and intimacy. You will want to balance both as you form a partnership with your leaders. Try to sit at a table; a large desk may be seen as a barrier between you and the table will give you both space to read or write. Position the chairs so that your leaders do not feel their personal space is invaded.

Eliminate Distractions. Try to eliminate interruptions such as phone calls, visitors, and visible reading and work materials. Provide quality meeting time, giving your full attention. This is related to the location challenge. When discussing your initial agreement, discuss muting the phone, BlackBerries, and even email prompts.

Eye Contact. Use appropriate eye contact. Be sensitive to cultural differences in what is considered appropriate eye contact. For example, in some cultures, averting the eyes during listening shows respect, and in others direct eye contact during speaking is appropriate.

Body Language. Keep an open body posture. Rest your arms casually at your side or on a surface, rather than folding them. Lean forward to display eagerness to hear what your leader is saying. Supplement your speech with appropriate facial and hand gestures. Show enthusiasm by nodding approval, smiling, or shaking the other person's hand. However, don't be artificial. Don't fidget. Eliminate any habits, such as clicking a pen, shaking your foot, or drumming your fingers.

1. Use Direct Communication

A coach must be flexible enough to select and use language that will be most effective with the leader. This begins by knowing the leader's communication style.

Interpersonal Style

An individual's preferred communication style affects interactions with others. For example, some leaders may prefer to intersperse business conversation with humor, while others may not. One leader may prefer to talk about the big picture before discussing details, while the other may prefer to get specific facts lined up before dealing with a large issue. Some leaders may focus on logic, while others focus on feeling.

Being aware of your leaders' communication styles and preferences is a critical factor in the comfort level of your meetings. You may discover differences in style gradually or you may compare notes from a communication style questionnaire or assessment tool. Either way, both of you should be conscious of style differences and be flexible in style practices in order to contribute to positive and comfortable communication. When coaches are open about an attempt to be flexible, they are modeling and may teach leaders to recognize the importance of flexible style in interactions with others.

Communicate Openly

Coaches need to be candid and direct when sharing their insights and feedback. The coach is primarily responsible for ensuring that the leader clearly understands the purpose for meetings, the rationale for leadership practices, the importance of the coaching relationship, and dozens of other things. This requires articulate, clear, and complete communication. A coach can't hide behind vague explanations, jargon, or poorly chosen words to avoid hurting the leader's feelings or fear of retribution.

2. Ask Powerful Questions

Coaches like to use the term "powerful questions" to define the kind of inquiries they make of their leaders. There is a good reason. Asking the right question may be one of the most powerful tools in your coaching toolbox. Why is that? Questions:

- Demonstrate that you are listening.
- Provide the means for gaining more information and knowledge.
- Strengthen a relationship because questioning shows you care.
- Clarify communication.

You have many kinds of questions to select from: rhetorical questions, reminding questions, feeling questions, thought-provoking questions, probing questions, reality-check questions, encouraging questions, and many others. In a coaching situation, asking questions is rarely about finding the correct answer; it is more about what your leader learns through the questioning process. Powerful questions are a successful link to that process.

What Are Powerful Questions?

Powerful questions help your leaders:

- Explore alternative solutions and ideas. This exploration helps them evaluate and consider the options available and make informed decisions.
- Make progress toward the ultimate goal and improve their leadership skills along the way.
- Discover different ways to consider how they see leadership and other aspects of their world.
- Take action and make decisions that move them closer to what they want.
- Gain insight into themselves.
- Gather more complete information faster.

Powerful questions generate creative thoughts and stimulate reflective conversations. Leaders turn powerful questions over and over in their minds and touch a deeper meaning. They are thought-provoking questions that may lead to thinking, behaving, and leading differently.

A master coach appreciates the benefits of asking questions over having answers. However, it is not just about asking questions. It is about asking questions that guide your leaders to empowerment—asking powerful questions.

Have you ever had an experience when someone asked you a question that just stopped you dead in your tracks? It made you examine a belief or a behavior in a different way? It may have been life-changing. That's a powerful question.

How to Ask Powerful Questions

To learn how to ask powerful questions, you have to start asking questions of any sort! A coach asks more questions, as opposed to stating ideas and opinions. How can you compose a powerful question? Try this process to help you craft powerful questions.

1. Begin questions with "what if," "why," or "how." Note this isn't a guarantee, but these questions will be more powerful than those that begin with "who," "when," or "where," or the least powerful, closed-ended questions, to which the leader responds with "yes" or "no." Take care with "why" questions so that they do not come across as confrontational.

2. Determine the purpose of your question. Powerful questions are most beneficial when they are relevant to the leader, authentic (you really do not know the answer), and generate a new way to view a current situation. Meaningful purposes could guide your leader to:
    *   Identify focus.
    *   Relate ideas and concepts to other ideas.
    *   Determine a deeper perspective.
    *   Clarify the reasons for making a personal change.
    *   Decide how to make better progress.

3. Broaden the reach of the question. Think in terms of opening the aperture of a camera. Rather than taking a snapshot of the person, open the lens to include more of the person's surroundings. Instead of asking a question about the leader, include his or her team or family, the organization, or perhaps the industry. Broadening the scope helps the leader broaden his or her thinking.

4. Plan for the function the question will serve. Will it open discussion? Will it create a breakthrough in thinking? Will it give the leader a push? Will it evoke a new response?

5. Tap into your leader's learning style. An auditory learner will resonate more easily with a question that taps into sounds, and a visual learner will react faster to a question that taps into pictures. Here are a few examples:
   - *Auditory:* What opportunities are knocking at your organization's door?
   - *Visual:* If you were able to picture a model based on the emerging opinions, how would it look?
   - *Kinesthetic:* How can you rise above this negative situation and move things around to ensure it doesn't occur again?

This does not suggest that powerful questions can be turned out cookie-cutter fashion using a recipe. They can't. In fact, the best powerful questions occur naturally. It does suggest, however, that coaches need to practice asking questions in other settings and that powerful questions do not need to be a hidden mystery.

Practice Powerful Questions

Start practicing now. Use the guidelines above to formulate powerful questions. Then find opportunities to practice. What opportunities do you have coming up, such as meetings, emails, or conversations, where you could practice asking powerful (or not so powerful) questions? Think of a recent experience when you made an assumption. Whether it was a correct or incorrect assumption doesn't matter. What questions could you have asked that may have ensured that your understanding was clearer, faster, deeper, or more profound? Observe others as they ask questions in the next meeting you attend. What kinds of questions seem to lead to the best outcomes, understanding, and results?

3. Use Active Listening Techniques for Clear Understanding

Listening is a critical skill in any role; it is one of the most critical coaching skills— probably one of the top two or three. This section presents ideas to improve your listening skills.

Check Your Listening Level

Before you continue forward, check your listening level. How would you rate yourself on the following key listening skills? Consider all situations—not just when you are coaching a leader. What's your level of expertise? High? Medium? Low?

_____ **Listen for main points.** I focus on the key ideas. I make a mental outline of the main points and relate other ideas to them.

_____ **Listen for the intent.** Every message has two parts, the content and the intent. I identify the intent by observing and interpreting the non-verbal messages and mentally compare them with the spoken words.

_____ **Listen for the entire message.** I listen for feeling as well as fact. I pay attention to emphasis and the kinds of words, phrases, or ideas used. I also notice any emotion-filled words. How the speaker was affected may be more important than the message.

_____ **Resist distractions.** I control as many distractions as possible by not taking phone calls or allowing interruptions during meetings. I focus on speakers' facial expressions and ignore outside interferences.

_____ **Use excess thinking time appropriately.** I do not let my mind wander while waiting to hear the rest of the message. People speak at a rate that is well over one hundred words a minute and think at four times that speed! I use my excess listening time to focus on the speaker.

_____ **Withhold judgment.** I limit emotional reactions and rarely get excited or angry about others' comments until I am sure I understand them. I do not immediately draw any conclusions about whether the meaning is "good" or "bad."

_____ **Prevent personal biases from interfering with the message.** I do not allow my personal prejudices or hot buttons to detract from understanding what the speaker is saying.

_____ **Summarize and paraphrase often.** I demonstrate understanding by rephrasing the speaker's ideas in my own words. I may summarize by saying, "Let me make sure I understand so far . . ." or "The way you see this is. . . ."

Did you find a few areas that you could improve? You don't need to be coaching a leader to practice your listening skills; you can begin practicing today in many personal and professional situations.

Listening: One-Way, Two-Way, All Ways

You often hear about the importance of two-way listening. However, sometimes in coaching situations one-way listening is an appropriate way to listen. One-way listening, also known as passive listening, occurs when a listener tries to understand the speaker's remarks without actively providing verbal responses. The listener may deliberately, or unintentionally, send *non-verbal feedback* through eye contact, gestures, smiles, and nods. However, there is no verbal response to indicate how the message is being received. One-way listening is appropriate if the leader wants to "air a gripe," vent frustration, or express an opinion and may not want or need a verbal response, rather the leader may only want you to serve as a "sounding board."

Two-way listening, also known as active listening involves *verbal feedback*. The tools in Table 8.1 can help a coach listen actively.

What Should You Listen For?

Of course you know that you need to be a good listener, but what should you be listening for? Well, first, it is not just the words. As a coach, you listen for both the content and the intent. You listen for the message. What are the words your leader is using? What is the leader trying to tell you? What is the meaning? Since the meanings of words are in people, not in dictionaries, ensure that you are both using the same meaning for the words. But that is not the most difficult part of listening.

Equally important is to listen for the intent behind the content. Listen for the true meaning of the message. Some people say you need to read between the lines. The intent can take many different directions and lead you on various roads. The intent can have a positive or a negative connotation.

Positive. The intent of the message may suggest positive facets that you can use to help move the leader forward. For example, you might hear a readiness to experiment with a new skill or a personal quality such as resourcefulness or resiliency that you had not heard before.

Negative. The intent of the message may imply negative overtones. These aspects may suggest that you need to explore the concern further by asking more questions (see the previous competency), by gathering more data, or by simply being silent to allow the leader to add more content. You may also hear self-doubts or fears about trying something new.

TABLE 8.1. LISTENING TOOLS

Technique	Examples	Advantage	Tips
Paraphrase	"As I understand. . . ." "So what you are saying . . . ."	Clarifies two-way understanding	Use often
Reflect Their Feelings	"Sounds like you. . . ." "That must have been . . . ."	Helps listener empathize	Avoid, "You shouldn't feel that way. . . ."
Express Your Feelings	"When you say that, I feel. . . ."	Helps break down barriers	Be honest and open
Ask Open-Ended Questions	"Why do you think . . . ?"	Promotes openness	Avoid "firing squad" or "interrogation" methods
Encourage Information	"Can you give me an example?" "What happened next?"	Identifies all the data	Listen for double meanings
Capsulize	"So the point is. . . ." "In a sentence. . . ."	Clarifies and organizes when speaker is rambling or uncertain	Watch for signs of disagreement
React to Strengths Before Concerns	"The upside of this is. . . ." "On the positive side. . . ."	Build trust to being open to other ideas	Use a well-placed pause between two views
Get Closure	"In summary . . . ." "In a nutshell . . . ."	Provides finality and completeness	Don't use too soon
Non-Verbal Response	Good eye contact; Nodding; Leaning toward person	Displays interest and encourages information giving	Eliminate distractions

Use the checklist in Table 8.2 to identify some of the positive and negative messages your leader may be trying to tell you. Add more to create a tool that is useful to you.

A coach listens completely to the entire message, what the leader is saying or not saying, staying focused on the leader's agenda. Good listening prepares the coach to reinforce, encourage, explore, delve deeper, support, summarize, or suggest what the leader needs in the moment.

TABLE 8.2. INTENT OF LEADERS' MESSAGES

Read between the lines and listen for the intent of the message.

Positive Intent	
Willingness to Move Faster	**Developmental Readiness**
• Flow of ideas	• Acceptance of weaknesses
• Eagerness to begin	• Response time to the unanticipated
• Excitement	• Understanding of personal strengths
• Desire or eagerness to try something	• High standards for improvement
• Hope about the future	• Positive expectations about life
• _____	• _____
Supporting Personal Traits	**Positive Relationships**
• Candor and honesty	• Accepts direction from others
• Generosity and caring	• Supports diverse colleagues
• Accountable for own actions	• Helpful attitude to all: customers, employees, colleagues, family
• Initiative and risk taking	• Interested in others
• Strength and maturity	• Respectful of diverse others
• _____	• _____

Negative Intent	
Negative Reactions	**Fearful**
• Emotional outbursts	• Asks multiple questions
• Blaming; does not accept responsibility	• Change in breathing
• Inconsistency between words/actions	• Speaks slowly, searching for words
• Displays envy or resentment	• Creates diversions, changes subject
• Immature or egotistical responses	• Uses clichés or common expressions
• _____	• _____
Confused	**Opposes the Process**
• Acts dumb	• Displays impatience
• Makes minimum progress	• Resists setting objectives
• Unable to share feelings	• Forgets to complete actions
• Resists suggestions with excuses	• Vague commitment comments
• Brags, boasts about unrelated feats	• Has "tried that before" comments
• _____	• _____

4. Communicate Persuasively Using Metaphors and Analogies

The first rule in communicating persuasively is to identify what is important to the person, and then spend time on it. In addition, when you speak, use tools such as metaphors and analogies to get your point across. Metaphors are comparisons that show how two things that are not alike in most ways are similar in one important way. For example, if you are working with a new leader who is overwhelmed, you might say it may feel as if "leadership is like drinking from a fire hose." The metaphor clearly defines what your leader may be feeling.

An analogy is slightly different in that, if there is a similarity or correspondence between dissimilar things, there is an inference that they will probably agree in other respects. For example, coaching is like a supermarket because you have lots of things to choose from; you should always go in with a plan; you visit once a week, but select things that will make a difference all week long.

The dictionary difference between a metaphor and an analogy isn't as important as the idea that you can use them to help your leader make a shift from current thinking or doing to what is desired in the future. Use metaphors and analogies to add interest to your discussions with your leaders, to encourage your leaders to think for themselves, and to give them concrete concepts to hold onto.

Telling stories is another powerful way to make your point and to persuade your leader. Use stories that are either first-hand experiences or that you can personalize in a way for your leader.

5. Exhibit a Variety of Response Techniques

How you respond to your leader is an important communication skill. There are dozens of ways to respond. The more options you have, the better able you will be to select the best one. Three responses you may not have considered are reframing, challenging, and no response at all.

Reframing

Reframing is a technique to help your leader broaden his or her perspective. It is an opportunity for the leader to step back and look at the situation from a different vantage point. It does not necessarily change the person's view of things, but may help to open his or her awareness of the situation. So, although the person may not change his or her mind, you can help the person see the situation differently. To help a person reframe, you might say:

- How might your boss look at that situation?
- If the roles were reversed, what might you have done?

Challenging

Challenging is the art of giving your leaders gentle nudges so that they can make progress. You may challenge a problem the leader is facing, repeat behaviors that prevent progress, underlying beliefs, internal struggles, resistance, ethical decisions, or others. Whatever the challenge, as a coach you must do it with respect, compassion, and the knowledge that it is a critical area that your leader must address.

No Response

Sometimes the best response is no response. A master coach knows when to simply listen. One of those times might be when the leader asks you for your opinion. This is a time to know when you should hold 'em and when you should you fold 'em! In most cases, your best response is going to be, "What do you think?" Coaching is rarely about your opinion. Certainly there may be times when your opinion is warranted, but it is usually more valuable to present facts and data.

If a leader presents a concern or issue that suggests a lack of self-confidence, take care that the leader is not just looking for an artificial self-confidence booster. Don't jump in and save the individual with, "Of course that was the right thing to do," especially if you don't know for sure.

➤ INTERPERSONAL PROFICIENCY

No matter how smart you are, how hard you work, or how many coaching certificates you have, if you lack interpersonal skills, you will not be a successful coach. Interpersonal skills refer to how well you relate to others. Interpersonal skills include communication, but go beyond that to seeing the other person's side of the situation, being able to read between the lines, resolving conflicts, and respecting diversity.

6. Able to Read Situations Using Observations and Intuition

Intuition is the ability to understand a scenario without any apparent physical rationale. If you've ever "had a feeling" or made a decision based on a "hunch," you were using your intuition. There are those who would argue that there were signs, perhaps subtle, but they were there. It may have just been a twitch of an eyebrow or a slight nod of the head, hints that were barely perceived. These hints are all around us every day. If you can read the energy in a room accurately, your brain is most likely taking in all the signs that define the energy: what is spoken, what is not spoken, body language, mannerisms.

If you are a self-professed people watcher, you have been in life-long training to read situations and people. This is helpful during coaching because you can use it to read your leader. It will help you determine whether your leader has had a good day or not, is fully open with you or not, is comfortable with the objectives you've established or not, trusts you or not, is ready for coaching or not. Often your intuition will send you cues when it is time to end the coaching relationship. A well-tuned intuition will serve you well.

7. Aware of and Open to the Leader's Entire Situation

Your leader does not work in your coaching vacuum. All leaders have many aspects to their lives. They have their own staff they are coaching. They report to a boss who has expectations. They have home lives and families, pets and cars, volunteer efforts and home responsibilities, and hundreds of other things that make them who they are.

A master coach takes into consideration the entire leader. So, although you may be coaching leaders to Challenge the Process, they have challenging processes at home. And although you may be coaching them to Model the Way for their employees, they also must consider how their superiors are modeling the way.

The element that you see your leaders in may be the one-dimensional world of work. You will be a better coach if you can help your leaders incorporate their entire lives into the coaching efforts. Of course, you will not pry into personal-life situations unless your leaders request help with them. It is helpful, however, to know how to provide them with skills to address stress, whether at work or at home. It is helpful to know whether they are balancing all aspects of their lives. Your results will be better.

8. Present Constructive Feedback

A key aspect of a coach's job is to provide authentic and truthful feedback to your coaching client. Indeed, this is one of the best tools you have to ensure that your leader grows and learns to be a better leader.

Giving Feedback

Feedback will most likely begin with the data from your leader's LPI. Review your leader's LPI Feedback Report before your feedback meeting to ensure that you know the areas of strength and the areas that need the most improvement. Begin to make connections between the areas. For example, if your leader is strong in "treats people with dignity and respect" and has a low rating in "gives people a choice about how to do their work," you might want to explore how the leader can build on the strength to do a better job of giving people a choice about how to do their work. Use this feedback to set useful objectives.

As time progresses with your leaders, you will most likely gather other feedback and performance data. As a coach, you give both positive and constructive feedback:

- Positive feedback to reinforce correct behavior.
- Constructive feedback to change behavior that needs to be improved.

Both types of feedback are critical to the leader's professional growth.

When giving constructive feedback, you'll use several communication checks. You will check for readiness beforehand to determine whether your leader is interested in receiving the feedback. The most effective results occur when your leader solicits feedback. You will check for clarity during the feedback process to ensure that your leader understands. You will also check for action at the end, making certain that your leader knows what to do about the feedback.

When giving feedback to your leader, concentrate on the behaviors that you would like the leader to do more of, do less of, or continue performing. It's good practice to provide feedback as a regular part of your scheduled meetings, based on individual needs and your leader's developmental activities.

Share the wisdom of your past experiences and insights as a seasoned coach. Make a point to relate learning experiences, special anecdotes, and lessons learned whenever appropriate. This information sharing strengthens a coach-leader relationship.

The Ten Commandments of Feedback

Much has been written about how to give feedback. It really comes down to ten vital features that can advance feedback, turning words into positive action. Effective feedback is

1. **Desired.** Give feedback that your leader wants. Feedback is always best received and most likely to be acted upon when the leader solicits it. This is, of course, the ideal. There will be many more times when you will need to initiate the discussion. When you do, open by asking whether your leader is open to hearing your thoughts. Doing so prevents most of the natural defensive reaction.

2. **Honest, concise, and direct.** Give concise, quality feedback. Use candid, honest words that are easily understood. Don't beat around the bush; be direct. Fewer, precise words delivered in a straightforward manner have more impact than more circuitous words.

3. **Specific and observable.** Focus the feedback on what, how, when, and how much. Tell the leader what you have observed, "I notice that when you speak about work, you go into great detail about how you think your team members should do their work."

4. **Sincere.** Be genuine and authentic in your feedback. It is always good to temper corrective feedback with positive comments; however, don't feel you need to do so every time if there is nothing to add.

5. **Achievable and actionable.** Feedback should be something that your leader can act on—something that is within his or her control. It should be laid out as a specific behavior that can be done differently, perhaps added to the action plan.

6. **Timed close to the action.** Provide feedback that is timely. Deliver your observations as soon after the behavior as possible. This helps your leader to remember the event, what happened, why it occurred, internal feelings, and thoughts. Give frequent feedback so your leader has a clear understanding of progress.

7. **Accompanied by support.** You and your leader are partners working together; be sure to ask your leader how you can support him or her in making changes.

8. **Clear about impact and consequences.** This is the "why." Your leader should know why this feedback is important to his or her growth as a leader. What impact does his or her behavior or lack of behavior have on others. When you forget to praise people for a job well done, they may think you don't care or, even worse, that you don't approve.

9. **Phrased as a statement.** Asking a question like "Do you believe that you follow through on commitment?" gives your leader the choice of responding yes or no. If you already know that he or she does not follow through, and the leader answers "yes," you will need to come back to declare your leader wrong. Don't get into this situation. Phrase your feedback as a statement.

10. **Not exaggerated, labeled, or judgmental.** Don't exaggerate by saying the leader "always . . .," use labels such as "inappropriate," or be judgmental by declaring a behavior is "wrong." It does not improve the feedback, but instead weighs it down with negative language.

Use the checklist in Exhibit 8.2 to remind you of the important elements of giving feedback.

EXHIBIT 8.2. TEN COMMANDMENTS OF FEEDBACK

Give feedback that is

- Desired
- Honest, concise, and direct
- Specific and observable
- Sincere
- Actionable and achievable
- Timed close to the action
- Accompanied by support
- Clear about impact and consequences
- Phrased as a statement
- Not exaggerated, labeled, or judgmental

Feedback Process

If giving feedback is difficult for you, consider using a formula to help you know what to say. The formula in Exhibit 8.3 provides the basic structure for feedback. You can plug in the exact example in your own words. For example, you might say, "When you discuss your leadership philosophy, I become confused about the opposing directions." Wait for a response and then suggest, "What if you wrote out all of the elements to determine whether there really is a conflicting perception? What's your idea?"

9. Confront and Manage Lack of Progress

You may find yourself confronting your leaders on a variety of things; however, lack of progress is one of the things that occurs most often. What can you do to help your leader move forward if he or she is not making progress? These questions may provide some initial suggestions.

- Is it a time issue? How can you help your leader manage time better? Is he or she working on the right tasks? Is he or she delegating?

EXHIBIT 8.3. FEEDBACK FORMULA

Use this formula when you prepare to give feedback.

"When you . . . " [Describe behavior.]
"I become . . . " [How it affects you.]
Wait for a response, since the person will be ready with a response.
"What if you . . . " [Specify change and how it will make a difference.]
"What's your idea?" [Listen and be prepared to consider alternatives.]

- Is it a lack of organization? How can you help your leader get organized?
- Is the objective too large? Can you break it down into smaller bites?
- Does the objective lack meaning to your leader? Does it need redefining? How well is the action connected to the leader's daily work?
- Is the objective obscure or too distant? How can you clarify the objective? Can you put a stake in the ground that is closer and achievable? Can you help your leader identify a series of milestones?
- Is the leader denying the benefits? What is your role to clarify the rationale?
- Is the leader unprepared for coaching? Is it your responsibility to prepare him or her? Is it time to end the coaching contract?

These are just a few of questions you can ask yourself to manage a lack of progress. It is important to have the conversation about the lack of progress with your leader as soon as you notice it. You might ask questions such as:

- How are you feeling about your progress?
- How do you feel about your goals? Are they still relevant?
- What actions have you taken since we last met that move you closer to your goals?
- What obstacles prevented you from moving forward since we last met?
- What can you do to prevent these obstacles from occurring again?
- How can we change your goals to make them more attainable?
- What if you completed this? How would it change the way people respond to you?

A Growth Idea for You

Conflict is all around all of us. As a coach, you may want to invest in your personal growth by learning the skills it takes to become a mediator. This is a step beyond simply bringing people together to resolve conflicts when they arise. As a mediator, you could arrange to sit down with disagreeing parties and help sort out their differences. Taking on this role will not only provide you with additional skills, but you will also garner respect and admiration from those around you.

10. Respect Everyone from Diverse Backgrounds

Respecting your leaders is a mental mindset that is basic for being an effective coach. If you cannot respect the person you will coach, you should probably turn down the assignment.

► BUILDING RELATIONSHIPS

Begin to build the relationship with your leader right from the start. Establish an agreement that addresses expectations and boundaries. Demonstrate confidence in your ability to help your leader and confidence in your leader's ability to become a skilled leader. Building relationships entails fostering collaboration and trust, providing support and challenging your leader to move forward, maintaining confidentiality, providing recognition, and helping your leader accomplish goals without telling him or her exactly what to do.

11. Foster Collaboration and Trust

Your ability as a coach to build trust and to foster collaboration begins with your level of dedication to the relationship-building process. You must show your leaders that you care about their situations and want to help them reach their full potential. You must mean it. Building trust is embodied in many of the competencies, but at the minimum it means that you:

- Will be available when your leaders need you.
- Maintain confidentiality in your conversations and work with your leaders.
- Provide support by listening, gathering resources, providing ideas, and celebrating when goals are achieved.

- Respect your leaders even though you may not agree with your leaders' views.
- Show empathy to demonstrate that you really care about them as individuals. Put yourself in your leaders' place to better understand what they may be experiencing.

Four ways to build trust based on an individual's communication/behavioral style are shown in Table 8.3, which presents the four basic styles and the general behaviors used to build and strengthen a trusting relationship.

It is important that you know your leaders' styles to be the most effective in building trust. As positive as each of the trust-building behaviors appears, they can be perceived negatively. For example, someone who values honesty and candor may perceive carefully chosen "approving and accepting" comments as couched, hiding something, or weak. Someone who values being approving and accepting of others may perceive "honest and candid" directness as harsh, insensitive, or uncaring.

TABLE 8.3. BUILD TRUST

Leader's Style	Behaviors	Quotes
Driver, Controlling, Leading-Oriented	Honesty and candor	"I say what I mean." "You will always know where I stand." "You can be straight with me."
Analytical, Processing, Task-Oriented	Dependability and trustworthiness	"I do what I say I will do." "I keep my promises." "You can count on me for accuracy."
People-Oriented, Amiable, Supporting, Collaborative	Approving and accepting	"I value people and diverse perspectives." "You can count on being heard without judgment or criticism."
Free Spirit, Expressive, Enthusing, Socializing	Accessibility and openness	"I'll tell you what works best for me." "Let's keep our agendas open." "Tell me what works best for you."

12. Support and Challenge the Leader to Stay Action-Oriented

As a partner to your leader, you will balance supporting and challenging him or her to maintain a forward motion to reach his or her goals.

Support might come in the form of:
- Brainstorming ideas for action.
- Putting your leader in touch with another leader.
- Role playing a scenario before your leader takes action.
- Celebrating a key accomplishment.

Challenge might require you to:
- Solicit ideas from your leader to create a better process.
- Confront your leader about why a deadline was missed.
- Dare your leader to hold him- or herself to a higher standard.
- Urge your leader to take on a difficult situation.

13. Build an Intimate Rapport and Maintain Confidentiality

During the course of the coaching relationship, your leader may present you with problems that stem from conditions outside of work or from conflicts at work. Your leader may also ask your advice about how to make certain decisions. Some of these decisions might be confidential in nature. As a coach, your success in these discussions will depend on how well you established a trusting and open relationship.

To create an intimate relationship, in which your leader feels comfortable bringing you his or her concerns, you will maintain confidentiality and show respect for your leader. Show respect by listening carefully and attentively to the leader, by not interrupting, and by asking how you can be helpful. In addition, you should never disclose personal information that the leader shares with you—ever.

Note: Generally, coaching sessions are confidential, even if they are paid for by the leader's company.

14. Provide Recognition That Encourages Skill Building

All of us need recognition and encouragement to continue to work on difficult goals. Building a portfolio of leadership skills is hard work. Leaders need recognition along the way. If they don't receive it, they are likely to fall back to their old ways.

How can a coach help a leader to stay focused and continue to move forward and build additional skills? Consider some of these tips:

- Keep the purpose in front of your leader.
- Remind your leader why he or she wants to acquire these skills.
- Target successes that are important to your leader early in the process.
- Celebrate milestones along the way using something that might be meaningful to your leader: a certificate, a humorous reminder, or a handwritten note of congratulations.
- Maintain attention to the coaching plan, where your leader has been, and all that has been accomplished.

15. Refrain from Giving Specific Advice

To Advise or Not to Advise

It is better to let the leader arrive at his or her own solutions. When you do this, your leader sharpens his or her problem-solving abilities. There will be many times when you give advice to the leader, and when you do, emphasize that this advice comes from your own perspective or experience.

When your leader asks you for advice, preface your statements with, "If I were in your situation, I would consider . . .," "From my experience . . .," or "The way I see this situation. . . . ." Saying it like this helps your leader understand that the advice comes from your perspective. It is still your leader's responsibility to decide whether or not to apply it. Your leader will need to make a choice before acting. As a coach, your job is to stimulate your leader's ability to identify solutions, solve problems, make decisions, and take action.

Indirect Approach

As a coach, there are times that you will use an indirect approach. The focus of this approach is to let the leader discover problems and work out solutions that best fit his or her needs. This approach places the responsibility for outcome directly in your leader's hands. It requires you to use active listening skills. While listening to the leader, refrain from passing judgment, accepting what your leader says without imposing your own values and opinions.

Make It Safe. Ensure that your leader feels comfortable and at ease. Show a sincere interest in your leader's interests. Make it safe for your leader to express him- or herself with phrases such as:

- "I see. Would you like to tell me about it?"
- "Would you help me to better understand your feelings?"
- "Tell me more about that."
- "Okay, what happened?"

Use Reflection. As part of the indirect approach, you can reflect on what has been said by your leader. An indirect approach does not mean that you are passive throughout the discussion. Any discussion, if it is to be productive, requires both people to speak. Reflect on the leader's statements by restating the key point(s). Make sure you really understand what the leader is trying to tell you. If you reflect back and your leader states that you have misunderstood, try again. There is no such thing as a "wrong" reflection—just unclear understanding. Get clarity.

Silence Is Helpful. It is not unusual to stop talking during a conversation to organize thoughts, focus opinions, interpret feelings, or simply catch your breath. Many people feel pressure to break the silence by saying something. At these times, don't try to anticipate the leader's feelings or thoughts. This can lead the conversation in the wrong direction. It is better to let the leader restart the conversation when ready and continue it at his or her own pace. This eliminates putting too much of your feeling and biases into the conversation and allows the leader to voice his or her own feelings and thoughts.

➤ DESIGNING DEVELOPMENTAL PLANS

This section addresses designing your leader's developmental plans. You know by now that you won't actually be designing the plan, but that your leader will complete the plan with you acting as a guide. It follows a similar pattern to one that a corporate trainer might follow: select data sources and methods, analyze and diagnose the needs of your leader, generate development opportunities, solve problems along the way, and create an action plan.

16. Select Appropriate Data Sources and Methods

You gather data in almost everything you do. You gather data before you take a trip or go back to college. You also use data to make decisions about which toothpaste to purchase or whether to fill the car with fuel now or later. Where you get your data and how you gather it is determined by you. One thing is certain: you use data that you are comfortable with and from a source you trust.

As a coach, you will have the data from the LPI available to you. You may also have an opportunity to gather additional data, depending on your situation. Additional data that may be available to you includes:

- Additional questionnaires from other sources, including internal employee satisfaction surveys or customer surveys.
- Self-assessments completed by your leader.
- Interviews with colleagues, supervisors, or direct reports.
- Direct observations such as the nature of the job site and how individuals interact on the job.
- Performance data reviews, which can be an unobtrusive way to identify trouble spots.
- In rare instances, knowledge tests may be available.

Why are you interested in gathering data for coaching your leader?

- It provides you with baseline information.
- It can pinpoint specific strengths and areas that need development.
- It becomes a valuable planning tool for your leaders to compare where they are with where they want to be.
- It may suggest the kinds of developmental options that would have the greatest impact.
- When compared at the end of the coaching process, it displays growth and progress.

17. Analyze and Diagnose Needs

As a coach, you will review the data you have gathered about your leader. In the case of the LPI, your data will be compiled and packaged for you to share with your leader. In other instances, you will need to analyze the data and diagnose what is available to you. As you sort through it, look for themes that suggest areas of strength for your leader and areas in which your leader can make improvements.

18. Generate Development Options

Provide the data to your leader before you begin to generate development options. Be authentic and sensitive to your leader's reactions. If you have never provided feedback as a coach, you may wish to practice with someone. Review the Ten Commandments of Good Feedback before your meeting.

As a coach, you may play the role of "door opener" to help your leader establish a network of contacts within as well as outside the organization. This role is useful when your leader needs to meet other people to spur professional or social development. As a door opener, you also open doors of information for the leader by steering him or her to appropriate resources.

Hundreds of developmental options exist. You can suggest several career-building activities such as those that may fall into these categories.

- **Enrichment:** Enhancing skills and responsibilities by seeking or accepting new tasks and assignments while remaining on the current job.
- **Reassignment:** Moving to another position with different duties, without a change in pay.
- **Job rotation:** Temporary or time-limited assignments into a variety of functions or related sub-specialties to give breadth of perspective.
- **Education or training:** Taking skill courses, enrolling in academic programs, or completing self-study activities.
- **Professional organization membership:** Participation in meetings; holding office; attending seminars, workshops, or conferences; reading periodicals.
- **Observation and discussion:** Participation in cluster groups, shadowing assignments, and interviewing others in the target occupation.

These developmental opportunities provide your leaders with structure to grow and learn new skills, but if they can't fit it into their schedules, they may not follow through.

A list of generic activities that are briefer can be found in the next chapter. They can be used as a springboard for you and your leader to begin thinking about what will be most useful to your leader's development. Most important is to determine what will fit into your leader's normal day-to-day activities, increasing the chance of completion.

Once you have customized ideas to the leader's needs, you will incorporate them into your leader's action plan.

19. Solve Problems

Leaders often present all kinds of problems to their coaches. You may be adept at resolving work-related problems; in addition, be prepared for personal problems. When a coach has built a strong, trusting, and confidential relationship with a leader, frequently the leader may feel comfortable sharing. The more serious and personal the leader's problem, the more cautious you should be about giving advice. Naturally, confidences should be maintained. Use considerable discretion in handling sensitive information, realizing that the leader may feel anxiety, apprehension, or fear about disclosing personal information to you. This is where trust really is a factor.

It is possible that the leader may become emotional during your discussion; let him or her work through the feelings. If the leader wants to discuss this, you should allow him or her to talk freely about it.

20. Create a Results-Oriented Action Plan

Create an action plan based on the information you have gathered about the leader, including the results of the LPI. Objectives and goals are written using the SMARRT formula. Help your leader identify and access different resources and ideas that develop skills to achieve the stated objectives.

Create an action plan that targets objectives that are most important to your leader. Relating early successes to your leader's priorities helps to ensure that your leader will stay active, involved, and committed to improvement.

Help your leader explore possible actions that will have the greatest impact on his or her priorities. Teach your leader how to brainstorm ideas. Encourage your leader to apply what is learned in one situation to others. This experimentation helps your leader own the new, changed behavior.

As you coach your leaders on how to think, learn, and develop professionally, attitude and style are often subtle subjects. You can model attitudes and style that will be helpful traits for your leader to observe. For example, ensure that your leader observes you demonstrating flexibility and variety in approaches to tasks or situations. This helps your leader understand the positive side of approaching the same task in a variety of ways.

You should not be the only role model that your leader observes. Recommend several role models for your leader to see in action. When possible, encourage your leader to attend various meetings or work groups to observe different leadership styles in different settings or situations. Use this to discuss the pros and cons of various leadership behaviors. Then help the leader create his or her unique professional identity.

➤ INSPIRING ACTION

Inspiring action requires that you determine what is compelling enough to move your leaders to do something. Remember, you are asking your leaders to change something that they may have been doing one way for a long time. In many cases you are asking them to:

- Change their leadership styles.
- Try something new.
- Experiment with a new technique.
- Communicate differently.
- Complete actions that lead to new behaviors.
- Present themselves differently to their employees, supervisors, or teams.

So you can see that you are, in fact, asking your leaders to stop doing something that they may have done all their lives and that feels comfortable and to do something that is different and most likely uncomfortable. You're asking a lot. You will need to determine what it will take to inspire action—what will compel your leaders to make a change in how they Model the Way or Encourage the Heart.

21. Recognize a Leader's Readiness for Coaching

If your leader is ready for coaching, your battle is more than half over. How do you know? How can you tell? Answer the following questions:

- How does your leader reply to feedback?
- How does your leader respond to your ideas?
- How interested does your leader appear when you discuss changing behaviors?
- How does your leader reply when you ask about objectives and development?
- How does your leader act when you bring up leadership areas that need improvement?
- How willing is your leader to learn?

If your leader is positive, open to new ideas, is excited about learning, and recognizes the gift of feedback, your leader is ready for coaching. In fact, the last question is truly key to your leader's success. Studies we conducted found that there is a positive correlation between learning and leading. People who are more frequently engaged in learning activities, no matter what their learning style, perform better as leaders. This is a powerful lesson. The more we seek to learn, the better we all become at leading.

On the other hand, if the leader is defensive, makes excuses, knows everything that needs to be addressed, is reluctant to discuss other thoughts or ideas, or is hard to pin down during planning, he or she is most likely not ready for coaching.

Can you prepare leaders for coaching? Yes, you can. The organization will determine whether it wants to invest time and resources in the individual.

22. Encourage a Leader's Progress Toward Achieving Goals

As a coach, you will request actions that move your client toward his or her stated goals. Follow up the next time you see your leader by asking whether he or she completed the actions he or she committed to during the previous meeting. This simple act demonstrates your commitment to followthrough—a skill that is often deficient in leaders. And when your leader achieves success, be sure to reward it.

Keeping your leader on track by monitoring the action plan and tracking actions and outcomes is one of the most powerful things you can do for your leader.

Do you receive too much positive feedback? It is highly doubtful. Encourage your leader by frequently providing positive feedback during an assignment or while he or she is working toward a goal. Positive feedback boosts morale, removes doubt, builds self-esteem, and gives the leader a sense of accomplishment. Focus on what your leader does well and relate those successes.

23. Motivate and Inspire Leaders to Do More Than They Thought They Could

Most leaders are highly motivated individuals with a thirst for success. You usually perform the motivator role only when the leader has a very difficult assignment and is afraid of failing. Through encouragement and support, you can motivate the leader to succeed. Your leaders will appreciate creative learning opportunities that inspire them.

Inspiring leaders to accomplish more than they think they can is arduous work. One thing you can do is to watch for, create, or negotiate opportunities for your leader that may not otherwise be available to him or her. Opportunities can relate directly to the objectives you have set or indirectly to the leader's overall professional development. A coach should provide as many growth opportunities as possible, with minimum risk. Opportunities might challenge and instruct and should never set the leader up for failure. New opportunities may increase the visibility of the leader. When your leader masters certain skills, identify challenges that require more responsibility. Continue to challenge your client's assumptions and find new possibilities for action.

24. Sustain a Leader During Setbacks

Sustain your leader by showing your support and making yourself available to him or her, especially during stressful periods. The leader who knows you are available will not be intimidated about asking questions and seeking your guidance. Sometimes helping your leader see an overwhelming task as manageable smaller tasks may be all the support needed.

Sometimes the setbacks are political in nature. As a coach, you can help navigate through the inner workings of the organization and decipher the unwritten politics for your leader. This insider knowledge is acquired over a period of time. The inner workings of any organization are the behind-the-scenes dynamics not always apparent, but crucial to know. The unwritten rules can include special procedures or guidelines that are not always documented, informal leadership roles, or policies under consideration.

You may also help the leader navigate in the "white waters" of change. How to deal with turmoil, downsizing, rapidly changing missions, and organization structures are issues that may be of great concern to the leader. They may appear as setbacks to a leader, as opposed to the changes organizations face. Hold your leader accountable even during setbacks, to make the point that these are a part of an organization's life cycle.

25. Evaluate Outcomes

Using the LPI provides a natural way to evaluate outcomes. However, there may be times when evaluating outcomes seems elusive. Measurements are available; you may just have to work harder to identify them. Although not scientific, you should always ask your leaders to evaluate their own outcomes. Ask, "On a scale of 1 to 7, how confident are you that you are making progress?"

More scientific data can be gathered over time by comparing:

- Employee survey data.
- Performance review scores.
- Turnover in your leader's department.
- Sales figures for your leader's group.
- Customer satisfaction.
- Amount of work churned out by your leader or his or her department.

Evaluation may entail assuring that leaders are learning as much as possible from developmental assignments. Learning from experience is not automatic. Leaders are likely to assess developmental assignments in terms of how well or easily they accomplished a project rather than in terms of what lessons were learned. To help the leader learn from experiences, try discussing the experience with the leader this way:

1. Ask your leader to provide a concrete, detailed description of the experience. Probe for specifics on what was done and how problems were handled, rather than generalizations of how it went.

2. Ask your leader to describe feelings about particular aspects of the experience. This is known as reflective observation.

3. Have the leader explain what lessons were learned in the process. This leads to generalizations about technique, politics, and interpersonal relations, working with the rules, organizational culture, management styles, and functional interrelationships.

4. Based on the insights expressed, ask the leader to discuss possible strategies for future behavior in similar situations.

➤ FACILITATING THE COACHING PROCESS

The steps in this section include the practical process actions you can take: establish a coaching agreement, set measurable objectives, manage the time and priorities, monitor and hold the leaders accountable, and link the coaching with other organizational learning efforts.

26. Establish a Coaching Agreement

One of the first things that you do as a coach is to establish a coaching agreement. Understanding what is required in your relationship with your leader is the foundation to reaching such an agreement. Clarifying your relationship and the coaching process will prevent heartburn later.

When establishing a coaching agreement, discuss specific parameters such as what is being offered, time commitment, responsibilities, expectations of each other, timeliness for meetings, schedules, and objectives, among other things. An example of a coaching agreement is presented in Exhibit 9.1 in the next chapter. This is also a good time to determine whether there is a good match between you and your prospective leader.

27. Set Measurable Objectives

You have built-in measures when using the LPI; your leader can work toward improving his or her scores for specific questions or areas in general, such as Enable Others to Act. If you go beyond the LPI and use other content, follow some of these suggestions. Remember, these objectives may become a part of the coaching action plan or your leader's individual development plan.

Help Your Leader Develop Career Goals

It is easier to begin by setting long-term goals, about three to five years out, and work backward. Identify short-term goals once you know what the long-term goals are. You have probably set SMARRT goals and objectives in the past. If not, here are the components:

Specific. Goals need to clearly define what the leader wants to achieve, using active verbs to indicate things you can do (see, name, demonstrate).

Measurable. You need to be able to count or determine with a yes or no whether something has been completed.

Achievable. The goal should be a stretch, but not so much that the leader cannot accomplish it in the allotted time.

Result-oriented. Concentrate on the *results* of the efforts, not so much on the *activities* that are required to accomplish them. Activities are determined after the goals are set.

Relevant. The goals must be appropriate and in tune with organizational needs, while moving the leader closer to the type and level of work that he or she finds challenging and enjoyable.

Time-bound. Plan an overall time frame for goals with interim milestones to ensure that the leader is moving toward these goals. It's important not to make goals too future-oriented.

Target Areas That Need Development

Review the LPI and other data to determine the specific areas in which the leader needs to improve. It is also important to target developmental areas the leader requires in his or her current position and those areas that are critical to future positions. Allow the leader to do as much of this as possible. Discuss with your leader the critical knowledge, skills, and attitudes that will be needed for effective performance in the future. Weigh these against what the leader already possesses.

Limited in number. Create several career goals to eliminate the possibility of the leader feeling trapped, but avoid setting too many goals at once. Concentrate first on setting goals that will help the leader accomplish what needs to be done immediately.

Flexibility. Ensure that the goals are not so rigid that adjustments cannot be made. Sometimes changes in the leader's interests or in the workplace require altering the goals.

28. Manage Time and Priorities

In the beginning, the most difficult aspect of coaching for leaders may be setting time aside for the coaching meetings when dozens of other priorities crowd their calendars.

In nearly all cases, however, if the coaching is tailored to the leader's needs and progress is made, all agree it is worth the investment.

Determine Success Indicators

The leader must have a clear vision of the desired results of the coaching and each developmental activity. Be sure that your leader can answer the question: "How will I know I've succeeded?" It's not important what indicators you use, except that these indicators must be measurable and meaningful. Once you have an action plan in place, it will be an enabler to move the leader toward the career goals that the two of you set.

Evaluate Progress

Your coaching meetings should be used to evaluate progress toward the goals. This will provide the opportunity to reflect on what has been learned and to make adjustments as necessary. Marking/celebrating progress as interim goals are achieved is a motivational factor.

Use Meeting Time Wisely

As with any meeting, an agenda or clearly stated purpose will help your coaching meeting to be productive. When setting up the meeting, determine the purpose in advance. This helps you:

- Allot an appropriate time frame.
- Come prepared.
- Avoid surprises.
- Determine whether the meeting was a success.

At the end of each meeting, plan when the next contact will be (if you are not on a regular schedule), and identify the purpose. Don't change the purpose of the meeting without mutual consent.

29. Monitor and Hold Leaders Accountable to Achieve Results

Monitoring and holding leaders accountable is one of the biggest issues faced by coaches. Consider four things: your leader's schedule, using an action plan, breaking actions into small steps, and how to build learning into your leader's average day.

Timing is often critical. Developmental opportunities provide your leaders with structure to grow and learn new skills, but if they can't fit them into their schedules, they may not follow through.

The best way to assure that goals are reached is to outline specific actions your leader wants to take in order to achieve them. The action plan should be your leader's plan, not yours. Develop the plan together during one of your coaching meetings. Placing specific steps with due dates on an action plan gives you and the leader a roadmap to stay on track to achieving results.

You may need to break some of the steps down into smaller, doable actions. For example, if your leader has to find opportunities to lead a team, you may need to help him or her to break it down into smaller steps such as:

- Identify who is in charge of the process-improvement efforts.
- Schedule a time to meet with the process-improvement department manager.
- Attend the meeting with the process-improvement department manager to determine what opportunities are available.
- Evaluate the opportunities, identifying the area for which you would be most qualified.
- Develop a plan for how you would fit the time required into your schedule.
- Meet with your supervisor to present your plan.

This may seem like excess planning, but when an individual completes each step, it builds momentum and provides a feeling of success.

Last, but perhaps one of the most important options, is to identify how your leader can build learning into his or her normal work day. Everyone is busy, so it may be a huge burden to add extracurricular activities to your leader's day if it is already jam-packed. To identify these opportunities, a coach must listen carefully and help the leader uncover them. For example, if a leader needs to practice talking about "future trends affecting work," he or she could schedule it into the weekly staff meeting. If a leader needs to "improve praising people for a job well done," the leader could carry ten pennies in a pocket as a reminder. Each time the leader praises someone, a penny is transferred to the other pocket. Perhaps a reminder pops up at 2:00 p.m. to count how many pennies are still left.

None of these ideas will be the final answer to holding the leader accountable, but they can help.

30. Link Coaching with Other Organizational Learning Efforts

Coaching is not done in a vacuum. Coaching is also not conducted primarily for the leaders—although they certainly are the biggest recipients of positive outcomes. Coaching provides an organization with a common language and consistency, developed leaders, an increased commitment and engagement by high-potential leaders, and employees who are ready to move into leadership roles with additional responsibilities.

This makes it imperative that you link your coaching with other learning events that are occurring in the organization. For example, if there is a mentoring program, how are mentors chosen and how do their responsibilities differ from those of a coach? If the organization sponsors academic opportunities, find out which ones are available for your leaders. If internal training is offered, find out how coaching is portrayed in the classes.

Finally, it is important that you know the overall philosophy of the leadership development program. Is the entire organization using *The Leadership Challenge* materials or are other efforts occurring at different levels or for different groups? To be successful, ensure that your coaching content is linked to the organization and its ultimate goals.

SUMMARY

As a role model, you are a living example of the values, ethics, and professional practices of the coaching profession. If you work internal to your organization, you also represent the values, ethics, and professional practices of your organization.

Most leaders, in time, imitate their coaches. If indeed "imitation is the sincerest form of flattery," then setting an example may be your most effective teaching tool. Your leader will learn a great deal about you while observing how you handle situations or interact with others. For this reason, you must be aware of how you come across to your leaders. Strive for high standards of professionalism, solid work ethics, and a positive attitude. Give your leaders an opportunity to learn the positive qualities of an exceptional, experienced professional.

Identify what your own position and career field require in terms of self-development. Demonstrate to your leaders what you have done and/or are doing to fulfill those requirements. Have you achieved certification? Taken post-graduate classes? Work these accomplishments into your discussions with your leaders. Even if you are in a different position from the one to which the leader aspires, your personal example is important.

Coaches must remember hundreds of things. Don't expect that you will be able to do everything at once. The next chapter presents a process you can use. It will be a reminder of some of the things you do throughout the coaching process.

CHAPTER 9: THE COACHING PROCESS

In This Chapter

- Introduce the 6Cs of Coaching.*
- Explore each of the 6Cs.
- Provide tips for implementing the 6Cs

In this book we have provided you an overview of The Leadership Challenge® Model, The Five Practices, and The Ten Commitments. We have introduced the concept of coaching and the competencies required to be an accomplished coach. Like any successful course of action, coaching follows a specific and repeatable process. The coaching process presented here, the 6Cs of Coaching, provides a roadmap for you to follow as you help your leaders move toward excellence.

Coaching cannot be framed in a neatly designed, paint-by-number picture. However, there are some guidelines that help coaching go more smoothly. The most successful coaching occurs in a repeated set of tasks that reflect the leader's learning and growth needs. Each task may require the coach to assume different roles.

While the tasks add more definition, try to think of them as an upward spiral in which the leader becomes more and more savvy and continues to gain more skills and knowledge. At the same time, the coach increases the challenges, expands the level of expectation, suggests more complex developmental strategies, and asks more thought-provoking questions. Much like leadership, coaching depends on building a relationship for successful results.

---

* © 2006, 2009 ebb associates inc. Used with permission.

FIGURE 9.1. THE 6CS COACHING PROCESS

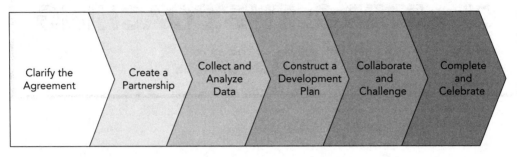

The 6Cs naturally cross over and blend into each other. For clarification, they are presented separately here to offer some structure.

THE 6CS OF COACHING TASKS

Like any repeatable process, coaching has specific steps that walk you from start to finish. The 6Cs of Coaching process incorporates the following steps, called tasks (see also Figure 9.1):

1. Clarify the Agreement
2. Create a Partnership
3. Collect and Analyze Data
4. Construct a Development Plan
5. Collaborate and Challenge
6. Complete and Celebrate

Task 1: Clarify the Agreement

In Task 1 of the coaching process, you will

- Build a relationship with the leader.
- Recognize whether the leader is ready for coaching.
- Establish a coaching agreement.
- Determine whether you and the leader are a good match.

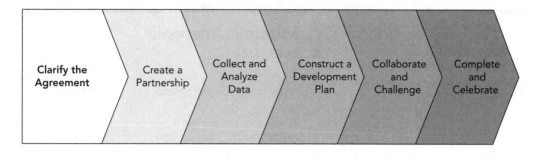

Task 1 provides you with the stepping-off point to prepare you for discovering more about the leader and the situation. Whether you are an internal coach or an external coach, you begin by building a relationship with the potential leader. As an internal coach, you bring knowledge of the organization and its jargon, processes, personalities, politics, operations, undiscussables, and many other aspects that an external coach may need to learn. As an external coach, you bring knowledge and ideas from other companies and leaders, as well as an open slate unfettered by any internal baggage.

Plan for your initial meeting. Establish a set of questions before the meeting to ensure that you obtain the information you need to learn about the leader. You might ask questions such as these:

• What do you hope to accomplish from coaching?
• What do you expect of me?
• How do you envision our meetings will go?
• What do you expect to happen between our meetings?

Completing a coaching agreement like the one shown in Exhibit 9.1 will help guide your discussion, but you should certainly add other questions and discussion points that you have found useful in the past.

Think in terms of the role you will play and what your leader needs to know. Does your leader know what the coaching relationship entails? Has he or she ever been in a coaching situation in the past? Does the leader understand that he or she holds the key to success? Or does the leader expect you to play the role of expert, deciding what needs to be done to improve LPI scores and prescribing solutions? Your first meeting is the best time to clarify your collaborative partnership role.

EXHIBIT 9.1. COACHING PARTNERSHIP AGREEMENT

Coach Name	Department/Organization	Telephone
Leader Name	Department/Organization	Telephone

What we believe the organization expects of us . . .

Logistics: How often shall we meet?   Who will initiate contact?
Where shall we meet?   How else can we connect?
How much time shall we make available?   Our first meeting will be:
How do we address cancelled meetings?

What the Leader expects from this partnership:

What the Coach expects from this partnership:

Guidelines that will help us work well together:

   Timeliness:

   Rescheduling:

   Meeting between scheduled times:

   Documenting actions and progress:

   Bringing closure:

Initial Objectives and Focus

1.

2.

3.

4.

How we will address issues that may arise, e.g., conflicts between us; one of us is not getting what we think we should; one of us thinks we are mismatched; lack of progress; gender, racial, or cultural issues.

We agree that our discussions are confidential:

Leader Signature	Date
Coach Signature	Date

The skills you need for the first meeting read like an "Interpersonal Skills 101" class. Here are a few that will help you.

- Observe the leader to determine whether to make small talk first or to get right down to business. Attending to the leader's communication style will lay a foundation for the rest of the discussion.
- Listen for understanding, especially to determine critical points. Sometimes a leader will not be clear about what he or she wants. Read between the lines and interpret meanings or structure content to make sense of the situation. Remember that every statement has at least two messages: the content and the intent.
- Ask pertinent and thought-provoking questions. Before you attend the meeting, develop three to ten questions based on what you know. Three well-thought-out questions will usually get the discussion started. You will probably not have time to ask ten questions, and if you have more than ten, it will be difficult to prioritize while you're trying to focus.
- Put your leader at ease by using his or her name, showing interest in his or her needs, and by balancing the discussion appropriately.
- Exude self-confidence without arrogance. You display your self-confidence with your body language as much as anything, so use good eye contact, a pleasant demeanor, and confident posture. If the leader is not familiar with your work, he or she may want to know about your past experience. Providing examples or relating similar situations should be a natural part of the discussion. Take care to avoid bragging, giving too much detail, or sounding as if you have rehearsed a rote speech.
- Project a professional image. First impressions count. A firm handshake, appropriate attire, and genuine interest in the leader help you make a great first impression.
- Be flexible. Adjust to changes and modifications that may occur during the meeting, clarifying at each juncture.
- Clarify expectations. Discuss the results the client desires.
- Take excellent notes, quoting what the leader says as well as your interpretations. Make notes to yourself about any follow-up that is required also.

In this step you will also consider your leader's readiness. How do you know whether your leader is ready for coaching? You will gain a sense of readiness as you work through your partnership agreement. Is he or she excited about receiving the LPI Feedback Report? Willing to make the coaching meetings a priority? Open to making improvements? Ready to try new methods and practices on the job? Interested in learning more about how The Five Practices offers a map to becoming an excellent leader?

Or instead is he or she reluctant about hearing the LPI data? Unwilling to commit to regular meetings? "Sent" to get coaching by a supervisor? Is excuse-filled, for example, "not my fault," "boss doesn't know anything," "overworked," "too many changes," "not appreciated." Any of these should be red flags that you might explore now or in a subsequent meeting. Don't make the decision about whether your leader is ready for coaching based on your first meeting only. His or her reactions might just be "first-time jitters." If negativity persists, explore it in more depth during a future meeting.

Try to reach agreement on basic expectations during your first meeting. Some coaching partners rely on just talking about these topics; others capture decisions in writing. Communication should lead to decisions about the following:

- Logistics such as meeting location, how often to meet, and for how long.
- Expected outcomes and measures that may be used.
- Format and expectations for documenting actions and progress.
- Confidentiality regarding data, discussion, and all other issues.
- Commitment expected, including time commitment, meeting cancellations, and others.
- Communication desires for the leader and the coach, such as candor or how to communicate between meetings.
- Role clarification.

These decisions may be made in one meeting or they may require more time. They may be verbal or they may be formally written in a Coaching Partnership Agreement like the one shown in Exhibit 9.1, your own form, or even an original document you draw up with each leader. You may not have time to discuss every item. That's okay, because it gives you a starting point for your next meeting.

Wrap up. Reiterate assignments, next steps, and timelines to ensure that both of you are on the same page. You should leave the meeting with a sense that you and the leader are a good match for what lies ahead.

Tips for Your Success

- Walk into your first coaching meeting with a very clear perspective of who you are, what values you espouse, and what you believe about coaching and leadership.
- Be yourself during the first meeting and you won't ever need to live up to anything else.
- Explain what you do in terms of your leader, not yourself, using "you" instead of "I." You might say, "If you are interested in being a better leader, coaching can help you by. . . ."

Task 2: Create a Partnership

In Task 2 of the coaching process, you will:

- Determine the needs of the leader to initiate and maintain a partnership relationship.
- Model being a good partner.

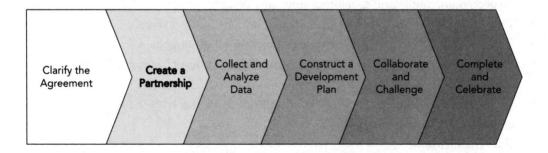

While this is Task 2, don't be lulled into a belief that this is something you do at this point in the process and never revisit again. In actuality, your partnership is the underlying foundation for your relationship. The stronger and deeper your base, the more powerful and resilient your relationship will be with your leader.

A partner role means that you and your leader balance responsibility throughout the experience from the beginning (when you define the agreement) through the end (when you measure the outcomes). There is a sharing of skills and knowledge, agreement on accountability, and concurrence on all decisions. This leader involvement increases consistent leader progress. A solid partnership creates a bridge between the leader and you, between the expectations of the leader's world and the knowledge and skills you can share with the leader.

In the early stages of the relationship, it is easy to allow the leader to depend on the coach for support and direction. And, although you may do more directing, advising, or teaching now than later, take care that you model your role as someone who helps the leader find answers from within. Depending on the situation, coaches may find that they need to focus more on building self-confidence at this time to balance the partnership. As you get to know each other better, other partnership-building skills will be required, such as being curious, flexible, present, and motivating.

The coach has the primary responsibility to model good partnership skills, including some of the following:

- Be flexible and adjust to your leader's preferred communication style.
- Respect diverse backgrounds.
- Refrain from coming up with all the ideas, developing all the solutions, and doing the work.
- Be prepared to inspire and motivate your leader during milestones and successes.

Tips for Your Success

- Initially take responsibility to manage time and priorities to keep things moving along; as the leader progresses, you can reduce your involvement in this area.
- Ask questions that address issues before they become issues, such as, "What's the best way to deal with you when you are resisting coaching?" or "What is your expectation of me when you are late for our meetings?"

Task 3: Collect and Analyze Data

In Task 3 of the coaching process, you will:

- Review the data available, such as the LPI Feedback Report.
- Decide what other data is required.
- Analyze all the information you have available.
- Provide feedback to the leader.

The Coaching Process

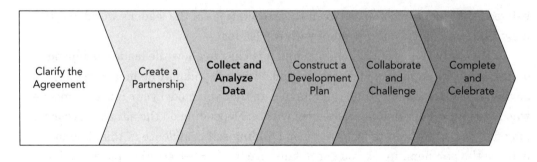

Clarify the Agreement → Create a Partnership → **Collect and Analyze Data** → Construct a Development Plan → Collaborate and Challenge → Complete and Celebrate

Once you have initiated a working relationship and have agreed on the next steps with your leader, it's time to gather data. You will most likely have the results of the LPI, but there may be other information that you want to collect from other sources, including internal employee satisfaction surveys or customer surveys; self-assessments completed by your leader; interviews with colleagues, supervisors, or direct reports; direct observations at the job; or performance data reviews. For example, if your leader scores very low in one of The Five Practice areas, you may want to identify some examples of behavior that may be causing the score. In other instances, you may want to gather information about the leader's communication style to help him or her understand how his or her behavior is perceived by others.

The ultimate goal of gathering data is to determine the current state and the desired state. The difference, or the gap between the two, is the change that must occur.

Several reasons for gathering data include the following:

- More clearly define the situation and the leader's needs.
- Determine root causes of the behavior.
- Determine the leader's preferred or desired future state.
- Provide baseline data.
- Specify the unique behaviors for improvement consideration.

You review and analyze the data looking for trends and messages you can share with your leader. When presenting the feedback, do so in a two-way conversation that may utilize the following question sequence:

- What themes do you see running through this data?
- What actions might cause people to provide this rating?
- What have you tried?

- What was the result?
- What do you suggest/recommend as next steps?
- How are you feeling right now?

Be prepared for unanticipated consequences and issues that may be uncovered during this discussion. A coach must objectively review the data and present it candidly and honestly. What you learn may direct you back to the beginning to revisit the intended objectives and goals—or even your agreement with the leader.

You will find dozens of suggestions and ideas for presenting feedback to your leader in Chapter 8, Coaching Competencies. Check for ideas there if you want more information.

Tips for Your Success

- Help leaders see the data as messages for their improvement; try not to focus on the numerical measures.
- Explore consistency from one data source to another and between those groups who responded to the LPI or other measures.
- Think of the data as a tool to challenge your leader's current mindset and to open a door that leads to envisioning a preferred future.

Task 4: Construct a Development Plan

In Task 4 of the coaching process, you will:

- Guide the leader to generate development options.
- Create a results-oriented action plan or development plan to use for monitoring and tracking results.
- Set measurable objectives.

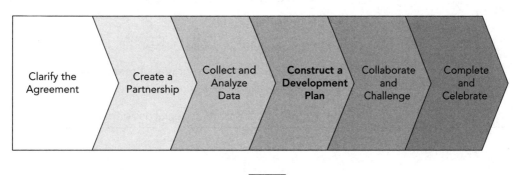

Clarify the Agreement | Create a Partnership | Collect and Analyze Data | **Construct a Development Plan** | Collaborate and Challenge | Complete and Celebrate

Research tells us that most learning occurs in informal settings and on the job. So the more you can do to develop learning opportunities that occur on the job the better. This also saves time for your leader. Chapters 2 through 6 are filled with developmental ideas that are related to The Five Practices.

In addition, Table 9.1 lists generic ideas that you can use. Many of them fit into a leader's day-to-day work. Your leader will be most successful if he or she selects or even creates the developmental activities that move him or her closer to the identified goals.

TABLE 9.1. DEVELOPMENT IDEAS

Personal Improvement: Opportunities that hone a leader's skills, address personality issues (this includes issues that may derail a career), and improve individual effectiveness.	• Join the mentoring program as a protégé • Maintain a leadership journal • Start a leadership reading club • Interview others • Observe others working • Help to plan special events • Teach a course • Read books, journals, and articles • Conduct research online • Read e-zines, e-newsletters, blogs • Gain experience as a volunteer in the community • Volunteer for your diversity council • Teach a course to other employees • Teach a course at a local university • Join Toastmasters • Complete Dale Carnegie classes • Volunteer to participate or lead a team effort, project, or assignment • Volunteer to conduct a special assignment

	• Participate in intern recruitment, job fairs, college visits
	• Assist another person to formulate an individual development plan (IDP)
	• Make it a practice to read at least two books every month
	• Observe a leader whom you respect and identify what makes that person a good leader
	• Complete self-analysis instruments such as the MBTI or styles instruments; obtain feedback on the results
	• Join a professional association
	• Attend conferences
	• Subscribe to a related professional journal
	• Present at a conference
	• Get involved in a community service
	• Become a mentor or coach to someone
Open Enrollment Classes: Sessions that may be offered internally or externally or, in the case of podcasts, on demand.	• Attend single university courses • Identify and register for the courses offered internally • Apply to external executive education programs • Apply to internal executive education programs • Attend targeted leadership classes such as The Leadership Challenge Workshop or those offered by a range of organizations (e.g., ATD, CCL) • Apply for advanced degree education • Consider e-learning opportunities such as webinars • Enroll in an internship program • Subscribe to podcasts • View blogs, wikis

(Continued)

TABLE 9.1. CONTINUED

Daily Experiences: Chance to experience short-term projects or processes that build skill without a great disruption in current job responsibilities.	• Request expanded stretch assignments • Play an "acting role" when the supervisor is away • Serve as a mentor • Volunteer for a hiring panel • Lead a new project • Be a "buddy" to a new employee • Work with an actively involved boss • Request on-the-job training to perfect skills • Role play with a colleague or the coach • Attend meetings as an observer • Ask for feedback from friends, colleagues
Organizational Job Assignments: Long- or short-term opportunities to experience a diverse set of scenarios, allowing the leader to gain organizational knowledge and to prepare for broader leadership roles.	• Tour other departments or locations • Participate on an organization-wide Six Sigma team • Assume lead person responsibilities • Join a team; lead a team • Switch jobs with a co-worker for a short period of time • Conduct a study of . . . • Volunteer for special assignments and projects • Lead a cross-functional team or task force • Shadow a leader in another department • Coordinate or report on a project to another department • Accept a job rotation • Work at headquarters for a time period • Connect with others through structured networking

Various Other Opportunities	• Coaching
	• Peer coaching
	• Reverse coaching
	• Career field mentors from other organizations
	• Sabbaticals
	• Loaned executive programs
	• Assessment centers

Once you select actions, write them as objectives that can be tracked and measured. Write the objectives using the SMARRT formula found in Chapter 8. Create a development plan by listing the actions on a coaching action plan like the one in Exhibit 9.2 or a format that you prefer. As a minimum, track a list of actions that are written in measurable, observable terms. Include the date that the leader wants to complete the objective. Identifying resources and obstacles at this stage of the process helps you and your leader think through the likelihood of meeting the deadline as well as what is required to actually complete the tasks.

The exact format for a developmental plan doesn't matter, but having a process to record plans and actions is important. This document will track progress. It is the way that you and your leader will monitor completed actions and measurable objectives. This document helps you hold the leader accountable for achieving success.

Tips for Your Success

- Find ways to encourage big ideas and dreams as you establish the development plan.
- Persuade the leader to find answers and seek challenges in the selection of learning options.
- Prod your leader into taking risks and trying things that are not typical for him or her.
- Suggest strategies and ideas that are new to your leader such as networking with other people or taking part in events that may be new to the leader.

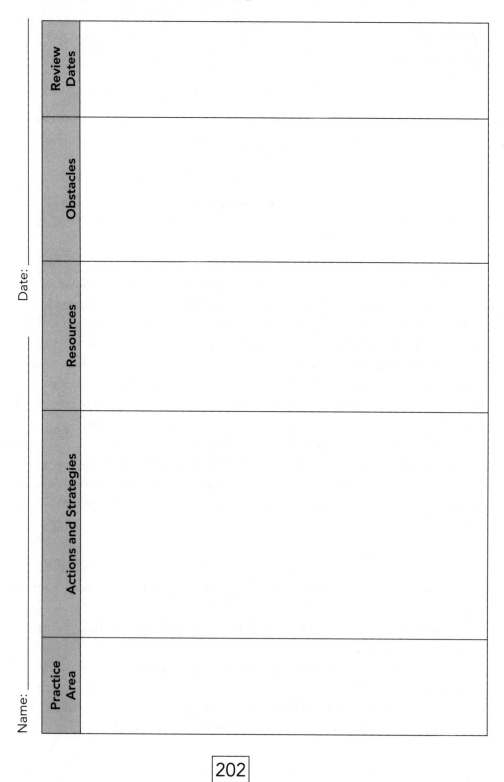

EXHIBIT 9.2. COACHING ACTION PLAN

Name: _____ Date: _____

Practice Area	Actions and Strategies	Resources	Obstacles	Review Dates

Task 5: Collaborate and Challenge

In Task 5 of the coaching process, you will:

- Find ways to keep your leader on track.
- Be available for your leader during setbacks and celebrations.
- Challenge your leader to accomplish all that is possible.

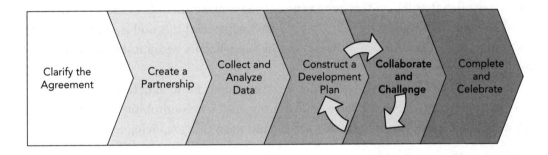

By the time you reach this task, you and the leader have had experiences that allow you to work together to jointly solve problems and field a few successes. You and your leader may experience this task for months, but during that time you and the leader should also experience the task at a higher level.

As your leader accomplishes some of the development opportunities, you both will actively seek other ways for him or her to grow and learn. Notice the added cyclical arrows on the 6Cs of Coaching process. This signifies that you will continuously cycle back to review the developmental plan in order to help your leader move to a more superior operating level. This is the collaborative, positive side of coaching, and during that time you may be:

- Building an intimate rapport and trust.
- Providing recognition and praise for completing actions and making changes.
- Encouraging your leader to take the lead in solving problems.
- Asking powerful questions that lead to insights.
- Using active listening for clear communication.
- Presenting constructive feedback.

In other instances, things may not be going as planned and you may be faced with more challenges. In this case you may be:

- Challenging the leader to complete actions.
- Asking powerful questions that challenge your leader's existing mindset.
- Confronting and managing a lack of progress.
- Sustaining your leader during setbacks.
- Motivating and inspiring your leader to do more than he or she thinks he or she can.

A recent survey of LPI coaches conducted by The Leadership Challenge, A Wiley Brand, revealed that follow-through is one of the greatest difficulties coaches have because leaders get caught up in the day-to-day responsibilities and lose sight of their leadership goals. Therefore, monitoring and holding leaders accountable to achieve results becomes a struggle.

Look to the previous task, Construct a Development Plan, to determine whether there was anything you might have done to prevent the accountability struggle. The following actions can improve accountability and keep things moving along:

- Don't overtax your leader's time.
- To monitor progress, create a practical action plan and discuss it at every meeting.
- Break the actions down into small, manageable steps.
- Rely on activities that can be built into your leader's work day.

The Collaborate and Challenge task is the longest-lasting of all the 6Cs. It grows and changes as your leader grows and changes. You will continually look for new and better ways to collaborate with your leaders and to challenge them to greater triumphs.

Tip for Your Success

- Stop looking at learning separately from working. As a coach, think of how it changes things if you view it as one thing: learning while working.

Task 6: Complete and Celebrate

In Task 6 of the coaching process, you will:

- Reach agreement with the leader that it is time to end the relationship.
- Bring closure to the formal relationship.
- Identify ways to celebrate success.

The Coaching Process

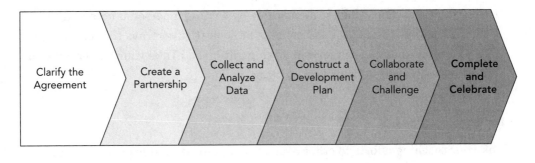

By this time, your leader has mastered most of the expectations originally identified by the two of you. However, as he or she continues to take on more responsibility, your leader may still require someone's wisdom and professional insight. One positive step the two of you can take is to ensure that you hand your leader off to a mentor who can continue to act as a sounding board and empathetic listener.

Here are some signs that it is time to end the relationship:

- You have reached the agreed-on end date or progress.
- Your leader has met all his or her identified goals.
- You are completing redundant "clean up" work.
- You have become friends with your leader and find yourselves discussing personal things more than business objectives.
- You determine that the leader needs a coach with a different skill set.
- You intuitively sense that the energy does not exist for one or both of you.

Whatever the sign, end the relationship by doing these five things:

1. Reach a mutual agreement that the end has come. You might ask, "Are we still making progress?" or mention observations you have made about progress in a specific leadership practice.

2. Identify what the leader needs so that you are not leaving him or her without support.

3. Review how far the leader has come and help him or her create a way to maintain the new skills and behaviors for the future.

4. Contract for the end by identifying undone actions and specifying a target date.

5. Celebrate the ending. Make it memorable by writing a personal note and/or giving a small gift such as a poster, mug, or book that portrays the relationship. (Check www.Baudville.com for reinforcing gift ideas.) Take your leader out to a coffee shop to celebrate your last meeting.

Tip for Your Success

• Link your coaching efforts to other aspects of organizational learning so that your leader understands the range of learning opportunities available to him or her.

SUMMARY

After working through the 6Cs of Coaching process, you can more easily see that, like leadership, coaching is a relationship.

The 6Cs of Coaching can serve as a reminder about the tasks that need to be completed to build the coaching relationship and to achieve results. They serve as a guide to use when helping a leader make sense of his or her LPI Feedback Report. The 6Cs will take you from "Hello, I'm your coach" to "Congratulations, you're an exemplary leader!"

CHAPTER 10: COACHING WHEN THINGS GO AWRY

In This Chapter

- Address things that can go awry during a coaching assignment.
- Suggest ideas for resolving and preventing problems.

Coaching is an exciting and interesting job; however, everything will not always be perfect. This chapter is dedicated to the unfortunate times when things seem just a little off, your leader isn't quite as motivated, or you are just not on top of your game. Let's explore a few things that can go awry, probable causes, and potential preventive measures.

WHAT'S THE BIGGEST CONCERN?

In 2008, The Leadership Challenge, A Wiley Brand, conducted a survey among the current LPI certified master coaches. Two items were repeated over and over as the biggest obstacles facing coaches:

- Leaders do not follow through with their commitments.
- Leaders have difficulty relating The Five Practices back to the organization and to life in general.

These related issues are certainly not a surprise. Everyone, and leaders in particular, is busier now than ever. When was the last time you took a vacation without taking your work? When was the last time you had white space under your emails? When was the last time you were in a meeting without your cell phone or

BlackBerry vibrating? When was the last time you left work on time every day of the week? When was the last time you had plenty of time for planning and reflection?

More to do and less time to complete tasks is a way of life. Coaches must accept that leaders do not have excess time to create new projects, to take more classes, to do more research, or to take part in many of the other learning events that are available—exciting learning opportunities, but time-consuming. In The Leadership Challenge, A Wiley Brand, survey, coaches stated that leaders "get caught up in the day-to-day work issues rather than focus on the key goals." "The biggest issue is always follow-through. Clients struggle with sticking to their commitments."

Given these issues, coaches have a two-fold responsibility to their leaders. They must help leaders select actions that are a part of their natural day, thus ensuring that they both:

- Save time, and
- Are relevant to work and life in general.

Look for ways your leaders can implement and or practice the desired skills by melding them into their natural workdays or with family and friends.

In this book we have suggested that you think of learning and work as one. If you stop thinking of learning separate from working and view them as the same, you will be able to be more creative as you work with leaders to determine how to build skills. And that is why this book provides you with so many options:

- Approximately two hundred activities relating to the thirty questions on the LPI to use as they are, as well as to inspire your own creative ideas.
- Almost one hundred books, articles, and websites for you to recommend to your leaders or to tap into for ideas.
- Almost two hundred questions you can ask your leaders that will act as a catalyst to provide self-insight.

This isn't necessarily easy; it *is* creditable. It requires diligent work by the coach. It requires skills that were discussed in Chapter 8, and it requires a coach who:

- Is creative.
- Isn't willing to give up.
- Understands how to ask questions that get at the underlying issues.
- Can translate ideas into practical tasks.

For example, if your leader is working on either (or both) "giving people a great deal of freedom and choice in deciding how to do their work" or "ensuring that people grow in their jobs by learning new skills and developing themselves," encourage the leader to carry a small notebook and pen in his or her pocket. When observing, working with, or talking with team members, the leader can jot notes about the kinds of skills required, who has a skill mastered that could be shared with others, and what employees need to learn to be able to make more choices in their jobs.

WHAT ELSE CAN GO WRONG?

As in any profession, things do happen that create barriers. Here are a few of those, with suggested questions you might ask to get things on track.

Tasks Are Appropriate and Still Not Completed

Sometimes you may have worked with the leader and selected activities that are a part of the natural work day and will not take additional time. The leader may still not follow through. What is happening here?

The leader may have different priorities. Perhaps things have changed in the organization or the department. Unknown to you, the leader is applying for a different position or considering leaving the organization. You'll probably want to ask, "I sense something has changed. Would you like to talk about it?"

Perhaps the goal and supporting actions are too big and overwhelming. Your leader has agreed to outline specific actions and how to achieve them. The action plan should be your leader's plan, not yours. Develop the plan together during one of your coaching meetings. Think back. Did you push too hard? Were deadlines too short? You may need to break some of the steps down into smaller, doable actions. You may ask, "What assignment will help you move toward your goal?"

The Leader Is Disinterested

Your leader may have new priorities, a new focus at work, a new job or job responsibilities. Maybe something is going on in your leader's personal life. Perhaps the leader has not seen any benefit in the coaching meetings. You might ask, "What are you avoiding?" or "What do we need to discuss?"

The Leader Is Unavailable for Meetings

You and your leader completed an agreement at your initial meeting. Bring it out during another meeting and ask for a commitment to scheduled meetings. You may need to learn whether something has changed since your initial agreement. You might begin the conversation by saying, "I've noticed that you have been unavailable for our last two meetings. Is there another time that works better for you?"

The Leader Is Negative

You have been working with your leader and he or she finds nothing positive to say is about anything. You might consider hitting it head-on and asking what it is like to have this type of outlook at work. You could also consider a discussion to identify affirming statements. Something that works well is to respond with: "Imagine that is possible. What would it take to make it happen?" (or whatever wording is appropriate). The response will most likely be negative. Just keep coming back with the same words such as, "You may be right that it isn't possible. Now imagine that it *is* possible. What would it take to make it happen?" Eventually the person will respond. Follow up by processing the discussion.

The Leader Resists

This depends on what the leader is resisting. Perhaps you missed something early in the relationship. If so, review the coaching partnership agreement. Ask whether your leader is willing to commit to the expectations and assignments. Listen for reasons for resistance and follow up with a related statement. Perhaps your leader is resisting because he or she just does not want to do something, such as holding a difficult discussion with an employee. You've done what you can to prepare the leader (in this case, you may have written out a mock discussion or role played the discussion). Ask what else the leader needs to be able to move forward. Sometimes rewards may motivate. You might ask your leader to imagine what it will be like once the difficult situation is over. You can even coach from the negative side by asking what is the worst thing that could happen or what if the situation were worse. Many reasons exist for resistance. That means coaches need many tools to help the leader break through it.

Your Leader Is Egotistical

Perhaps you are working with a leader who really does not think he or she has any issues. Your first task is to determine whether your leader really believes he or she has the skills or if he or she is trying to conceal a lack of self-confidence. Use the data from the LPI or other instruments to help with your discussions. Confirm strengths and ask questions that reach deep inside and help to pull out answers that the leader may not have wanted to face. Pose some "what if" questions, such as, "What if your weaknesses were your strengths?" "What if the data are correct? How would you approach it?" "What if the data belonged to your best friend? What would you tell her to do?"

Your Leader Responds Emotionally

Every so often you may touch on a topic that hits a chord with your leader. The response could be anger, sadness, or fear. Be sure to first acknowledge the emotion. Follow this by stating the effect the emotion has had on the session and discuss whether you both want to continue. If you decide to continue, propose how you can both refocus on the topic you were discussing. Be sure your leader knows that your support continues.

IS YOUR LEADER READY FOR COACHING?

Ideally, the leader will desire a coaching experience. He or she understands what it will entail, is open to feedback, and will be consistent with follow-through. However, not everyone can handle coaching or even wants it. You will only be able to tap into a leader's potential if you are working with an individual who wants you to.

At times you may be assigned to leaders who are not ready for coaching. Perhaps they are negative about the idea of having a coach. Perhaps they lack confidence in themselves or are withdrawn. Perhaps they are overconfident in what they can do. Whatever the cause, you might wonder whether a coach can prepare leaders for coaching. The answer is usually yes, you can work with them to prepare them for a coaching experience.

Try these strategies to start:

- Facilitate a discussion about what coaching is/is not.
- Work through the partnership agreement to uncover any questions the leader may have.
- Suggest that you try a minimum number of coaching sessions and then revisit the leader's concerns.
- Discuss commitments of roles, responsibilities, scheduled meetings, and coaching assignments. Then ask how the leader feels about these commitments.
- Discuss the benefits of data gathering and how the feedback can support the leader's goals.

SHOULD YOU EVER END A CONTRACT EARLY?

Coaches, both internal and external, are reluctant to end a contract early. However, there are times when it must be done. It may be more difficult if you are an internal coach because you may still work in the same building every day. In addition, people will be curious about what happened. There are often warning signs that something is amiss. Heed these leader behaviors and, when necessary, end the arrangement. Here are some of the warning signs:

- Forgets the specifics of your partnership agreement.
- Changes commitments you both agreed on.
- Postpones meetings, activities, and other events.
- Has unrealistic expectations.
- Does not appear to be committed to the outcomes.
- Puts off obtaining information.
- Is too busy for meetings.
- Disregards or discounts your suggestions and recommendations.
- Appears to have a hidden agenda.

If you need a quick check to determine whether the situation needs further consideration, use Exhibit 10.1.

EXHIBIT 10.1. SOMETHING'S AMISS CHECKLIST

How Do You Know Something Isn't Right?

- Leader cancels meetings.
- Leader is distant or disinterested.
- Leader makes excuses.
- Leader doesn't complete tasks.

PROBLEMS ARISING WITH OTHERS

Your leader may encounter negative attitudes of others who believe that he or she is getting ahead by association with you rather than by advancing on personal merit. To prevent this, ensure that others see your leader's competence and abilities, not just your coaching relationship. Do not let your coaching efforts diminish the leader's sense of self-respect.

You may also find that the leader's supervisor is concerned about the coaching relationship. Try to assure him or her that your actions and suggestions on the leader's behalf do not undermine the supervisor. Keep the supervisor involved and informed as appropriate.

In both of these cases, it may be helpful for you to role play possible scenarios with your leader so he or she has some ideas of how best to respond.

TOUGH CONVERSATIONS

Communication is the key in all of these situations. In some cases, they may feel like difficult conversations. In all such discussions, the coach weighs carefully all of the options and maintains a balance between some seemingly disparate characteristics. During these conversations, the coach will most likely need to:

- Be sincere and caring, yet have a strong personal will.
- Listen carefully, and be ready with a powerful message when the time is right.
- Have ideas and solutions, yet refrain from giving direct advice.

- Push ahead through difficult comments and be willing to say "stop" when necessary.
- Display respect for the leader, while not necessarily agreeing.
- Desire success, but be willing to accept defeat.

None of these incongruent behaviors is easy for anyone. They are even more difficult for a coach working to improve another person.

After a difficult conversation, find another coach whom you trust. Debrief the scenario, asking for feedback and suggestions. This ensures that you continue to learn and grow and helps to build your own skills as a result.

IT'S ALL GOOD

Yes, there will be times when things go wrong. As a catalyst, coaches can make significant changes in their leaders' lives. Leaders need to move outside their comfort zones, sometimes even to the edge of their capacity. This is critical for growth. It isn't easy for the leader or the coach. It is, however, worth it. It's all good.

CHAPTER 11: COACH YOURSELF TO MASTERY

In This Chapter

- Become a master coach.
- Explore lifelong learning.
- Create a master coaching development plan.
- Identify personal development strategies.

You'll be busy being a coach for your leaders' development. However, don't forget about your own professional development. Remember the leadership challenge to DWYSYWD (Do What You Say You Will Do) pertains to coaches, too. Coaches must continue to learn and improve because they must be proficient in many topics. In addition to understanding The Five Practices and all of their nuances, you should also be well-versed in the LPI. But that's just content—the "what." You also need to be a skilled coach. That means understanding the coaching process from establishing needs through gaining results.

But a master coach has other skills as well: a vast number of communication skills, building relationships, creating partnerships, and motivating and inspiring leaders. This is no cookie-cutter job. Every day is different. Every leader is different, every design is different, and every organization is different. As coaches we are lucky to have these differences because they challenge us to grow and develop.

This is what makes the job of coach so exciting, but it is also what necessitates that you become a lifelong learner.

This chapter offers a list of ways that you can master the coaching process. It also suggests ideas for creating your professional development plan. Thomas Jefferson said, "If we did all the things we are capable of, we would literally astound ourselves." Most of us may never know all that we are capable of. However, becoming a lifelong learner is a step in this direction. Go ahead. Take Jefferson's challenge. Learn all you can. Do the things you are capable of. Astound yourself!

YOUR LIFELONG LEARNING AND DEVELOPMENT ARE CRITICAL

You know your development is important. Unfortunately, many of us get wrapped up in the day-to-day world and forget our own development—much like the old adage of the shoemaker's children going barefoot.

Develop your skills and knowledge to maintain your place on the cutting edge. By doing so you are providing the kind of coaching your employer and your leaders expect and deserve. Even more importantly, you owe it to yourself to continue to develop your skills and increase your knowledge. Staying in touch with the changes and the excitement of coaching will keep you enthusiastic and passionate about what you do. We should all enjoy what we do and have pride in ourselves and our profession. Coaches should not have to get up and go to *work* in the morning. Coaches should all love their jobs so much that they get up and go to *play* every day.

Becoming a lifelong learner keeps you vibrant and knowledgeable about the work you do. As a coach, your learning has three focuses: content, process, and personal development. Interestingly, both the subject of leadership and process of coaching are continually growing and changing.

The subject of leadership continues to develop and change as many experts at universities and organizations such as the Center for Creative Leadership conduct research. We continue to examine our model to ensure that it is contemporary in content and valid across a wide variety of audiences.

The process of coaching is relatively new as a profession. As Coutu and Kauffman (2009) say in a recent *Harvard Business Research Report*, "Coaching as a business tool continues to gain legitimacy, but the fundamentals of the industry are still in flux." This is a strong caution for you, as a coach, to stay in tune to developments and changes in the field of coaching.

Finally, your personal development, becoming a lifelong learner, ensures your success. Learning is paramount in order to achieve all that you are capable of.

What are the descriptors of a lifelong learner? Well, they are some of the same descriptors of being a coach. You become a lifelong learner by:

- Assessing where you are compared with where you want to be and determining a plan to get there.
- Improving your processes continuously. Identify new ways that are better and more efficient and implement them.
- Being on the cutting edge of the coaching industry trends. You are aware of state-of-the-art practices as well as the fads of the day; have knowledge of the professional coaching organizations and their philosophies; and read journals, e-zines, blogs, and newsletters that keep you abreast of the field.
- Being in the know about your clients (internal and external). You keep up-to-date about all the things that are critical to your leaders pertaining to their jobs, as well as new developments about leadership.

How do you stack up against the four things that lifelong learners do? You have an obligation to your employer and the leaders you coach to improve your knowledge and skills continually. In addition, you owe it to yourself to improve. The rapid changes in the fields of coaching and leadership make this an imperative move for you. What can you do?

CREATE YOUR MASTER COACHING DEVELOPMENT PLAN

You know that being a lifelong learner is important, but how do you get started? Who better than a coach to create a professional development plan? If you are already coaching, you probably help leaders think through and create their individual development plans. If you work internally, your organization most likely expects you to create your own professional development plan.

Contemplate the present. Think about where you are and where you want to be. Make a list of all the things you would like to learn—professionally and personally. Determine measures of success, specify your goals, and identify strategies to get there. Capture your desires in your developmental plan. Consider several strategies. Your development plan helps you stay focused. The next sections of this chapter present several strategies that you can include in your plan to improve your coaching knowledge and skills; improve your leadership knowledge and skills; and enhance your interpersonal ability.

IMPROVE YOUR COACHING KNOWLEDGE AND SKILLS

Knowing how to coach is critical. You can't read one book and expect to be a proficient coach. The following learning strategies and ideas can help you refine what you already know about being a coach or be suggestions for learning new techniques.

Take a coach to lunch. This strategy is a good place to begin if you are new to the coaching field. Invite someone who has been coaching for some time to lunch and ask him or her about the job. Some of the questions you might ask include these:

- How long have you been a coach?
- How did you get into the coaching field?
- Why did you decide to become a coach?
- What kind of coaching do you do? What do you do for your clients?
- How did you gain the skills and knowledge to be a coach?
- What was your greatest lesson(s) learned?
- What is the greatest challenge for you as a coach?
- What situations are the most frustrating for you?
- How can I best prepare myself to become a coach?
- What would you miss most if you stopped coaching?

Study with a master coach. Look for someone in your organization who can "coach" you. If there is no one inside your organization, look outside. Have the individual observe you working with a leader (with the leader's permission, of course) and give you feedback. Perhaps there will be an opportunity for you to observe the other person as well. Be sure to select someone with whom you can confidentially share your goals and aspirations, as well as your failures and competency needs. You will grow immeasurably with this single action.

You may wish to go to the Worldwide Association of Business Coaches (WABC) website (www.wabccoaches.com) or the International Coach Federation's (ICF) website (www.coachfederation.org) and click on "find a coach" at either website to locate a coach who has credentials. This certifies that the person has coached a required number of hours and has been recommended by other certified coaches. Here are other options to find a coach:

- Other coaching programs that are accredited by ICF will likely have their own databases of coaches. For example, The Coaches Training Institute (www.coactive.com) has a list at "find a coach."

- You could join a coach exchange program, a group where several people want to coach each other to gain experience or create your own with other coaches you know.
- You may be able to locate individuals currently enrolled in a certification program who are searching for clients. They may be willing to charge lower rates to acquire the number of coaching hours required by their programs.

Find your own coach. Identify something in which you would like to become proficient. Identify someone you respect who is accomplished in the area. You may want to learn to play tennis, to bake bread, to practice yoga, or one hundred other things. Discuss what you would like to learn from the other person and schedule two or three coaching sessions with the individual. After each session, write your thoughts and feelings about what you learned, how you learned it, and what you learned about the process of coaching.

Consider certification. Certification or accreditation is available in many fields as a way of learning and achieving a professional standing. The field of coaching is no different. The International Coach Federation (ICF) is the world's largest resource for coaches. Formed in 1995, today the ICF is the leading global organization dedicated to advancing the coaching profession. ICF sets high professional standards, provides independent certification, and builds a network of credentialed coaches. It is considered to be the authoritative source on coaching information and research.

ICF's Accredited Coach Training Programs are offered by numerous universities, colleges, and other organizations where you can learn a process to coach others, acquire useful tools, learn the principles behind coaching techniques, and practice coaching situations. Go to www.coachfederation.org for additional information. The concepts in this book have been based on ICF's core competencies.

Other organizations certify coaches, too. One you may wish to consider is the Worldwide Association of Business Coaches.

Take a coaching class—even if you have a certification. You will always learn something new from a coaching class. The Association for Talent Development (ATD) offers a two-day Coaching Certificate class. It is taught by individuals who have been coaches. The Center for Creative Leadership (CCL) offers a three-day Coaching for Development class.

Many of the organizations that deliver content for the coaching certification also offer individual classes. Consider ATD (www.td.org), CCL (www.ccl.org), Coaching U (www.coachinc.com/coachu), the Career Coach Institute (www.careercoachinstitute.com),

1 to 1 Coach Training (www.1to1coachingschool.com), and, of course, the International Coach Federation (www.coachfederation.org) or the Worldwide Association of Business Coaches (www.wabccoaches.com).

Observe a pro in action. Visit a pre-season football camp, a baseball spring training, or a practice session of your local ballet or orchestra. What does the coach or the conductor do that you could transfer to your work as a coach?

Co-coach with others. We are fully aware of the ethics of confidentiality, yet we do know that with your client's approval there may be times that you could bring in a second pair of ears and eyes. Coaching with a colleague is a unique way to learn from someone else in the profession. It allows you to observe someone else, elicit feedback, and learn from the experience of working together. Invite a coaching colleague to observe you during a coaching meeting. Ask for feedback about specific things. Sit down afterward and listen to everything your colleague says. Ask for suggestions for improvement.

Network. Sometimes a professional organization will provide a networking list of contacts in your geographic location. If not, form your own network of coaches. Plan to get together at least once each month. Meet for lunch or breakfast. Keep it informal, but have some focus each time. It could be a very simple "go around the table to state what has become clear in the past month" or everyone brings a tip about a specific topic. Networking is one of the best ways to continue to learn or, at the very least, to learn what you ought to learn! It will also provide you with names of people to call when you need support or guidance.

Explore and list your coaching ethics. If a reporter from *The New York Times* pushed a microphone in front of you and asked you to state your ethical beliefs about coaching, could you spew forth exactly what you believe? Take time to research the International Coach Federation's ethical guidelines. Then create your own ethics statement that you can easily share with anyone.

Professional coaching standards. Establish professional standards for yourself that are high enough to keep you on your coaching toes and position a bar that encourages continual reaching. You can again use the International Coach Federation's Professional Standards to start. Guarantee that your coaching will be the highest quality your leaders have ever experienced. Put quality ahead of everything else—you won't go wrong. Set your standards high and never compromise them. Call your professional standards what you like—a philosophy, a belief statement, your guiding principles—that doesn't matter. As a coach, spend time identifying what you believe equates to high-quality standards. Quality: first, last, and everything in between.

Discover resources. Visit your local bookstore. Browse the shelves looking for new coaching books. Look for topics about the trends in the industries you serve and business in general. Thumb through all new books about coaching to determine whether they should be on your bookshelf. Sign up for an online service. The World Wide Web is a dynamic source for professional development resources. Search for "coach" and you will find at least 56,000,000 sites. Sites provide information as well as link you to other related sites. Sign up for newsletters and webzines about coaching. Look for blogs related to coaching. For example, are you aware that we have a blog that addresses Leadership Challenge topics?

Peruse the reading list. A reading list at the end of this book offers suggestions for books to read. It includes both new coaching books, hot off the press, as well as several classics and standbys used by the best coaches in the world.

Get involved. Do more than just write a check for your annual coaching association dues. Volunteer for a committee. You will be involved in the work of the association, communicating with other professionals, and working with colleagues in your profession. It's an enjoyable way to continue to learn from each other.

IMPROVE YOUR LEADERSHIP KNOWLEDGE AND SKILLS

Leadership is an evolving topic, partially due to what we learn about how to lead, but also due to changes in the economy, the environment, generations, and many other things that affect our processes. You who coach leaders need to stay in touch with leadership thought leaders. These strategies help you do that.

Read Additional The Leadership Challenge–Related Resources. If you like this book and the philosophy it espouses, you may wish to read additional materials focused on *The Leadership Challenge*. Check out some of these.

- *The Leadership Challenge* (6th ed.)
- *Credibility: How Leaders Gain It and Lose It, Why People Demand It*
- *A Leader's Legacy*
- *Encouraging the Heart: A Leader's Guide to Rewarding and Recognizing Others*

- *Christian Reflections on The Leadership Challenge*
- *The Leadership Challenge Workbook*

Complete your own LPI. If you would like to receive feedback on how you are doing, check out the *Leadership Practices Inventory*, a 360-degree assessment offered either online or by mail. Even better, have a coach share the results with you. Observe the coach's techniques. Make note of the techniques that were helpful to you.

View a video. Several videos are available on *The Leadership Challenge Facilitation Set*. Observe them with a fellow coach to learn and understand more about The Five Practices. You can find more information about this resource at www .leadershipchallenge.com.

Attend learning events. At a minimum, attend your professional organization's annual conference. It may be expensive, but you owe it to your clients to invest in yourself. I can think of no more enjoyable way to learn than to go to a great location, meet new people, renew past acquaintances, and attend sessions in which presenters discuss new ideas and approaches. You may very likely go home with a fistful of business cards from others whom you can tap into to continue your learning.

To get the most out of your attendance, be sure to network. Don't sit on the sidelines or retreat to your room during breaks. You will not gain all the value that you can. Instead, go where the action is. Be the first to say hello. Introduce yourself to others and be interested in who is there. Identify common interests and experiences.

Attend virtual learning events. My email box is filled with offers to "attend" online seminars and webcasts. Many are free; the rest have a small price tag. All will stimulate learning, produce knowledge, and encourage your thinking.

Study on your own. Reading is a favorite method of learning. Get on mailing lists to stay up-to-date about the most recent coaching and leadership publications. Subscribe to and read your professional journals. Read general business magazines such as *Fortune, BusinessWeek,* or the *Harvard Business Review.* Read the same publications your leaders read to keep yourself informed about the industry. Read the cutting-edge journals such as *Fast Company.*

ENHANCE YOUR INTERPERSONAL ABILITY

Interpersonal proficiency is critical for almost all professions, but especially so for a coach. A coach's success depends on the ability to relate, communicate, and partner with leaders and others he or she coaches. It is critical to doing the job. Thousands of things exist that you could do to improve your interpersonal prowess. Here are just a few strategies.

Improve your communication skills. The skill that is most important to good coaching is communication. Unfortunately, the skill that goes awry the most often in coaching is communication. Your abilities to listen, observe, ask questions, give feedback, identify differences, summarize, and report objective information are important to master coaching. Equally important are your abilities to persuade, offer empathy, solve problems, and build trust. Each of these and many other communication skills are requirements for a successful coach. Continually work at improving your communication skills.

If you like being a coach, don't stop there. Be a master coach. Be a *respected, knowledgeable* coach. Be a *successful* coach. Be a *highly professional* coach. Be all the things that you are capable of being. *Astound* yourself!

Go back to school. You may not need an M.B.A., but courses at the graduate level are critical. Take courses related to what your leaders do: business, human performance technology, or organizational change. Take courses to improve your interpersonal skills: communication, partnering, emotional intelligence, or presentation skills.

Ask others. Ask for feedback from others on a regular basis. Ask for it from friends, colleagues, and your clients. Ask your leaders about their most pressing concerns. Although this is not related to you specifically, the learning may be fascinating, and this will enhance your relationship.

Keep a journal. Take about ten minutes each day to record what you learned that day. Also note what you wish to repeat and what performance you want to correct. For example, an entry might say, "Met with Mason today and was easily distracted by the other things I needed to do before the end of the day." This allows you to review these events at a later time to determine whether you need to structure a plan of action or you have changed/improved your behavior.

Observe people. You are surrounded by people every day. Start watching them, especially their facial expressions. What does it tell you about someone's temperament, communication style, or mood? If you can overhear their conversations, what can you observe about the mental models they use to form opinions? If you observe their dress and behaviors, what might it tell you about their profession or their next engagement?

Create mentoring opportunities. Identify someone in the coaching field whom you would like as a mentor. Then ask the person if that would be possible.

You might be able to meet your mentor for breakfast four to six times each year. You pay for breakfast and it will become the best $20 investment you ever made. You are investing in yourself. Identify where the experts hang out. Then go there. Sometimes this is a related association or an informal group. More seasoned people and those with different experiences can offer you priceless advice.

ASPIRE TO THE BEST YOU CAN BE

Your leaders expect you to be the best coach as well as knowledgeable about leadership. You owe it to them and to yourself to learn and grow. Learning is a lifelong process, even if you are at the top of your profession. Often it is what you learn *after* you know it all that counts!

It's not just what you know, but how you come across. Are you enthusiastic? Do you show genuine concern for the leader? Are you sincere? Are you respectful? Are you open to others' ideas? Are you confident? Are you excited about your leaders? Are you excited about what you do? Are you passionate about coaching? Do you aspire to be the best that you can be?

Find the excitement in your life. Find the passion in what you do. Coaches need be passionate about what they do and how they do it. You need to love what you do and do what you love. Becoming a lifelong learner is exciting. It puts passion back in your life! Remember, this is an investment in you. If you won't invest in you, who will?

Identify what it takes to master the art of coaching. Then coach yourself to mastery!

Reference

Diane Coutu and Carol Kauffman. "What Can Coaches Do for You?" *Harvard Business Review*, January 2009.

READING LIST FOR COACHES

Coaching

Adams, M. (2009). *Change Your Questions, Change Your Life: 10 Powerful Tools for Life and Work.* San Francisco: Berrett-Koehler.

Blanchard, K., and D. Shula (2001). *The Little Book of Coaching.* New York: HarperCollins.

Bolton, R. (1979). *People Skills: How to Assert Yourself, Listen to Others, and Resolve Conflicts.* New York: Simon & Schuster.

Buckingham, M., and D. Clifton (2001). *Now, Discover Your Strengths.* New York: The Free Press.

Carson, R. (2003). *Taming Your Gremlin: A Surprisingly Simple Method for Getting Out of Your Own Way.* New York: Quill/HarperCollins.

Coach U Inc. (2005). *Coach U's Essential Coaching Tools: Your Complete Practice Resource.* Hoboken, NJ: John Wiley & Sons.

Coach U Inc. (2005). *The Coach U Personal and Corporate Coach Training Handbook.* Hoboken, NJ: John Wiley & Sons.

David, M. (1999). *Coaching Illustrated: A Proven Approach to Real-World Management.* San Francisco: The Mark David Corporation.

Flaherty, J. (2005). *Coaching: Evoking Excellence in Others.* St. Louis, MO: Butterworth-Heinemann.

Goldsmith, M., L. Lyons, and A. Freas (2000). *Coaching for Leadership: How the World's Greatest Coaches Help Leaders Learn.* San Francisco: Pfeiffer.

Haneberg, L. (2006). *Coaching Basics.* Alexandria, VA: ASTD Press.

Hargrove, R. (2008). *Masterful Coaching* (3rd ed.). San Francisco: Pfeiffer.

Hargrove, R. (2007). *Masterful Coaching Fieldbook* (2nd ed.). San Francisco: Pfeiffer.

Hargrove, R., and M. Renaud (2004). *Your Coach in a Book*. San Francisco: Jossey-Bass.

Kirkpatrick, D. (2005). *Improving Employee Performance Through Appraisal and Coaching* (3rd ed.). New York: AMACOM.

O'Neill, M. (2000). *Executive Coaching with Backbone and Heart: A Systems Approach to Engaging Leaders with Their Challenges*. San Francisco: Jossey-Bass.

Peddy, S. (2001). *The Art of Mentoring: Lead, Follow and Get Out of the Way* (rev. ed.). Corpus Christi, TX: Bullion Books.

Peterson, D., and M. Hicks (1996). *Leader as Coach*. Minneapolis, MN : Personnel Decision Inc.

Whitmore, J. (2002). *Coaching for Performance: Growing People, Performance, and Purpose* (3rd ed.). Boston: Nicholas Brealey.

Whitworth, L., K. Kimsey-House, H. Kimsey-House, and P. Sandahl (2007). *Co-Active Coaching: New Skills for Coaching People Toward Success in Work and Life*. Mountain View, CA: Davies-Black.

General Leadership

Badaracco, J. (1997). *Defining Moments: When Managers Must Choose Between Right and Right*. Boston: Harvard Business School Press.

Bennis, W. (1994). *On Becoming a Leader*. Reading, MA: Perseus.

Burns, J.M. (1978). *Leadership*. New York: HarperCollins.

Collins, J. (2001). *Good to Great: Why Some Companies Make the Leap and Others Don't.* New York: HarperCollins.

Collins, J., and J. Porras (2004). *Built to Last: Successful Habits of Visionary Companies*. New York: HarperBusiness.

Gardner, H. (2011). *Leading Minds: An Anatomy of Leadership*. New York: Basic Books.

Gardner, J. (1990). *On Leadership*. New York: The Free Press.

George, B. (2004). *Authentic Leadership: Rediscovering the Secrets to Creating Lasting Value*. San Francisco: Jossey-Bass.

George, B., with P. Sims. (2007). *True North: Discover Your Authentic Leadership*. San Francisco: Jossey-Bass.

Kouzes, J.M., and B.Z. Posner. (2017). *The Leadership Challenge, Sixth Edition*. San Francisco: Jossey-Bass.

Kouzes, J.M., and B.Z. Posner (1993). *Credibility: How Leaders Gain and Lose It, Why People Demand It.* San Francisco: Jossey-Bass.

Peters, T. (1992). *Liberation Management: Necessary Disorganization for the Nanosecond Nineties.* New York: Knopf.

Pfeffer, J., and R. Sutton. (2006). *Hard Facts, Dangerous Half-Truths, and Total Nonsense: Profiting from Evidence-Based Management.* Boston: Harvard Business School Press.

Schein, E.H. (2017). *Organizational Culture and Leadership* (5th ed.). San Francisco: Jossey-Bass.

Leadership Development

Conger, J., and B. Benjamin. (1999). *Building Leaders: How Successful Companies Develop the Next Generation of Leaders.* San Francisco: Jossey-Bass.

Kotter, J.P., and D.S. Cohen. (2002). *The Heart of Change: Real-Life Stories of How People Change.* Boston: Harvard Business School Press.

McCall, M. (1998). *High Flyers: Developing the Next Generation of Leaders.* Boston: Harvard Business School Press.

Charan, R., S. Drotter, and J. Noel. (2001). *The Leadership Pipeline: How to Build the Leadership Powered Company.* San Francisco: Jossey-Bass.

Goleman, D., R. Boyatzis, and A. McKee. (2002). *Primal Leadership: Realizing the Power of Emotional Intelligence.* Boston: Harvard Business School Press.

Senge, P., A. Kleiner, C. Roberts, R. Ross, and B. Smith (Eds). (1994). *Fifth Discipline Fieldbook: Strategies and Tools for Building a Learning Organization.* New York: Currency/Doubleday.

Schwartz, M.K. (Ed.) (2000). *Leadership Resources: A Guide to Training and Development Tools* (8th ed.). Greensboro, NC: Center for Creative Leadership.

Tichy, N., with E. Cohen. (1997). *The Leadership Engine: How Winning Companies Build Leaders at Every Level.* New York: HarperCollins.

Websites

www.1to1coachingschool.com

www.aceproject.com

www.amanet.org

www.coachfederation.org
www.coachinc.com/coachu
www.franklincovey.com
www.goalmaker.com
www.lifeplanwriter.com
www.walkthetalk.com

INDEX

Page references followed by *fig* indicate an illustrated figure; followed by *e* indicate an exhibit; followed by *t* indicate a table.

Index

Blanchard, K., 111

Blogs/Websites resources: Challenge the Process, 78; Encourage the Heart, 127; Inspire a Shared Vision, 55–56; Model the Way, 35

Body language: ability to perceive, 164; eye contact form of, 153, 158; non-verbal communication using, 153

Book recommendations: Challenge the Process, 76–77; Enable Others to Act, 100–101; Encourage the Heart, 125–126; Inspire a Shared Vision, 54–55; Model the Way, 33–34

Book a Visit activity, 73

Brand You activity, 32–33

Bring Your Hobby to Work Day activity, 89–90

Bugs Me List activity, 67

Build a Playground activity, 66

Build Your Team activity, 87

Building Consensus activity, 28–29

Building Relationships: building rapport/maintaining confidentiality, 171; fostering collaboration and trust by, 169–170, 170t; providing recognition to encourage skill building, 172; refraining from giving specific advice, 172–173; supporting/challenging leader to stay action-oriented, 171

BusinessWeek, 222

C

Calendar/scheduling sources, 25

Call a Customer, or Two activity, 67

Carnegie, D., 112

Cashman, K., 46

Catch 'em Exemplifying a Value activity, 120

Caution Your Tongue activity, 84–85

Celebrate Success activity, 124–125

Celebrate Values and Victories: activities for, 124–125; being personally involved, 108; benefits of, 107; coaching tasks related to, 204–206; creating spirit of community, 107–108; team activities for, 124–125. *See also* Praising activities; Recognizing Contributions

Chair a Committee activity, 63

Challenge the Process leadership practices: description of, 3, 5, 6; experiment and take risks commitment for, 8, 10, 56–60,; how the

coach models this practice, 78; *Leadership Challenge Journal* kept on, 83; *Leadership Practices Inventory* (LPI) relating to, 60–75; references recommended to facilitate, 76–78; searching for opportunities commitment for, 8, 9, 57–58, 60

Challenge Thinking activity, 74

Challenger coaching role: communications related to, 146–147; description and functions of, 143*fig*, 144

Challenging communication response, 162

Change Website activity, 68

Check Yourself activity, 85

Checking Listening level, 157

Clarify Values commitment: description of, 8, 9; Model the Way by, 18–19

Climate of trust, 80

Coach Me, Coach You activity, 100

Coach modeling: of Challenge the Process practices, 78; for coaching The Five Practices of Exemplary Leadership, 134; of Enable Others to Act practices, 102–103; of Encourage the Heart practices, 127; of Inspire a Shared Vision practices, 56; of Model the Way practice, 35–36. *See also* Five Practices of Exemplary Leadership

Coach roles: advisor, 143*fig*, 144, 146; challenger, 143*fig*, 144, 143; consultant, 143*fig*, 145, 143; helper,143*fig*, 147–148, 144; orchestrater, 143*fig*, 145–146

Coach self-assessment: attitude and attributes, 141; characteristics, 140–141; process of conducting a, 141; skills and competences, 140, 150*e*–151

Coaches: aspiring to be the best you can be, 224; benefits of coaching for, 136; creating your master coaching development plan, 217; improving your coaching knowledge and skills, 218–221; internal versus external, 137–139; lifelong learning and development of, 216–217; many roles of, 143*fig*–148; mentoring opportunities for, 223–224; reading list for, 225–228; self-evaluation of abilities as, 61–64, 150*e*–151; similarities between exemplary leaders and exemplary, 3–4. *See also* Leaders; Resources

Coaches Training Institute, 132

Index

ABOUT THE AUTHORS

Jim Kouzes and Barry Posner have been working together for more than thirty years, studying leaders, researching leadership, conducting leadership development seminars, and serving as leaders themselves in various capacities. They are co-authors of the award-winning, best-selling book *The Leadership Challenge*, now in its sixth edition. Since its first edition in 1987, *The Leadership Challenge* has sold more than two million copies worldwide, and it is available in twenty-one languages. It has won numerous awards, including the Critics' Choice Award from the nation's book review editors and the James A. Hamilton Hospital Administrators' Book of the Year Award; has been named a Best Business Book of the Year (2012) by *Fast Company*; and was selected as one of the top ten books on leadership in Jack Covert and Todd Sattersten's *The 100 Best Business Books of All Time*.

Jim and Barry have co-authored more than a dozen other award-winning leadership books, including *The Truth About Leadership: The No-Fads, Heart-of-the-Matter Facts You Need to Know*; *Credibility: How Leaders Gain and Lose It, Why People Demand It*; *Encouraging the Heart: A Leader's Guide to Rewarding and Recognizing Others*; *A Leader's Legacy*; *The Student Leadership Challenge*; *Extraordinary Leadership in Australia and New Zealand: The Five Practices That Create Great Workplaces* (with Michael Bunting); *Turning Adversity into Opportunity*; *Finding the Courage to Lead*; *Great Leadership Creates Great Workplaces*; *Making Extraordinary Things Happen in Asia: Applying The Five Practices of Exemplary Leadership* (with Steve DeKrey); and *The Academic Administrator's Guide to Exemplary Leadership*.

They also developed the highly acclaimed *Leadership Practices Inventory* (LPI), a 360-degree questionnaire for assessing leadership behavior, which is one of the most widely used leadership assessment instruments in the world. More than seven hundred research studies, doctoral dissertations, and academic papers have used The Five Practices of Exemplary Leadership framework they developed.

Jim and Barry have received the Association for Talent Development's highest award for their Distinguished Contribution to Workplace Learning and Performance. In addition, they have been named Management/Leadership Educators of the Year by the International Management Council, ranked by *Leadership Excellence* magazine in the top twenty on its list of the Top 100 Thought Leaders, named among the Fifty Top Coaches in the United States (according to *Coaching for Leadership*), ranked as Top 100 Thought Leaders in Trustworthy Business Behavior by Trust Across America, listed among *HR* magazine's Most Influential International Thinkers, and included among the list of today's Top 50 Leadership Thinkers by *Inc.* magazine.

Jim and Barry are frequent keynote speakers, and each has conducted numerous leadership development programs for corporate and for-purpose organizations around the globe. These include Alberta Health Services, ANZ Bank, Apple, Applied Materials, Association of California Nurse Leaders, AT&T, Australia Institute of Management, Australia Post, Bain Capital, Bank of America, Bose, Camp Fire USA, Charles Schwab, Chevron, Cisco Systems, Clorox, Conference Board of Canada, Consumers Energy, Deloitte & Touche, Dow Chemical, EMQ Families First, Egon Zehnder, Electronic Arts, FedEx, Genentech, Google, Gymboree, Hewlett-Packard, IBM, IKEA, jobsDB Singapore, Johnson & Johnson, Kaiser Foundation Health Plans and Hospitals, Korean Management Association, Intel, Itaú Unibanco, L.L. Bean, Lawrence Livermore National Laboratory, Lockheed Martin, Lucile Packard Children's Hospital, Merck, Monsanto, Motorola, National Head Start Association, Nationwide Insurance, NetApp, Northrop Grumman, Novartis, Nvidia, Oracle, Petronas, Pixar, Roche Bioscience, Siemens, Silicon Valley Bank, Telstra, 3M, Texas Medical Center, TIAA-CREF, Toyota, United Way, Universal Orlando, USAA, Verizon, Visa, Vodafone, Walt Disney Company, Western Mining Corporation, and Westpac. They have lectured at more than sixty college and university campuses.

JIM KOUZES

Is the Dean's Executive Fellow of Leadership, Leavey School of Business at Santa Clara University, and lectures on leadership around the world to corporations, governments, and nonprofits. He is a highly regarded leadership scholar and an experienced executive; *The Wall Street Journal* cited him as one of the twelve best executive educators in the United States. In 2010, Jim received the Thought Leadership Award from the Instructional Systems Association, the most prestigious award given by the trade association of training and development industry providers. He was listed as one of *HR* magazine's Most Influential International Thinkers for 2010 through 2012, named one of the 2010 through 2016 Top 100 Thought Leaders in Trustworthy Business Behavior by Trust Across America and honored as one of its Lifetime Achievement recipients in 2015, cited by the Association of Corporate Executive Coaches as the 2015 International Executive Coach Thought Leader of Distinction, and selected by Global Gurus as one of the Top 30 Leadership Gurus in 2015. In 2006, Jim was presented with the Golden Gavel, the highest honor awarded by Toastmasters International. Jim served as president, CEO, and chairman of the Tom Peters Company from 1988 through 2000 and prior to that, he led the Executive Development Center at Santa Clara University (1981–1988). Jim founded the Joint Center for Human Services Development at San Jose State University (1972–1980) and was on the staff of the School of Social Work, University of Texas. His career in training and development began in 1969 when he conducted seminars for Community Action Agency staff and volunteers in the war on poverty. Following graduation from Michigan State University (BA degree with honors in political science), he served as a Peace Corps volunteer (1967–1969). Jim can be reached at jim@kouzes.com.

BARRY POSNER, PH.D.

Is the Accolti Endowed Professor of Leadership at the Leavey School of Business, Santa Clara University, where he served as dean of the school for twelve years. He has been a distinguished visiting professor at Hong Kong University of Science and Technology, Sabanci University (Istanbul), and the University of Western Australia. At Santa Clara he has received the President's Distinguished Faculty Award, the school's Extraordinary Faculty Award, and several other teaching and academic honors. Barry has been named one of his nation's top management/leadership educators by the International Management Council, recognized as one of the Top 50 leadership coaches in America and Top 100 Thought Leaders in Trustworthy Business Behavior, ranked among the Most Influential HR Thinkers in the world, and listed among the Top Leadership and Management Experts in the world by *Inc.* magazine. An internationally renowned scholar and educator, Barry has authored or co-authored more than one hundred research and practitioner-focused articles. He currently serves on the editorial advisory board for the *Leadership & Organization Development Journal* and the *International Journal of Servant-Leadership* and received the Outstanding Scholar Award for Career Achievement from the *Journal of Management Inquiry*.

Barry received his BA with honors in political science from the University of California, Santa Barbara; his MA in public administration from The Ohio State University; and his PhD in organizational behavior and administrative theory from the University of Massachusetts Amherst. Having consulted with a wide variety of public and private sector organizations worldwide, Barry also works at a strategic level with a number of community-based and professional organizations. He has served on the board of directors of EMQ FamiliesFirst, the Global Women's Leadership Network, the American Institute of Architects (AIA), Big Brothers/ Big Sisters of Santa Clara County, the Center for Excellence in Nonprofits, Junior Achievement of Silicon Valley and Monterey Bay, Public Allies, San Jose Repertory Theater, Sigma Phi Epsilon Fraternity, as well as publicly traded and start-up companies. Barry can be reached at bposner@scu.edu.

ELAINE BIECH

Is president and managing principal of ebb associates inc, an organization development firm that helps organizations work through large-scale change. She has been in the training and consulting field for thirty years and works with business, government, and non-profit organizations.

Elaine specializes in helping people work as teams to maximize their effectiveness. Customizing all of her work for individual clients, she conducts strategic planning sessions and implements corporate-wide systems such as quality improvement, reengineering of business processes, and mentoring programs. She facilitates topics such as coaching today's employees, fostering creativity, customer service, time management, stress management, speaking skills, training competence, conducting productive meetings, managing change, handling difficult employees, organizational communication, conflict resolution, and effective listening.

She has developed media presentations and training materials and has presented at dozens of national and international conferences. Association for Talent Development (formerly ASTD) has referred to Elaine as the "trainer's trainer." She custom designs training programs for managers, leaders, trainers, and consultants. To date, Elaine has designed, developed and piloted five certificate programs for ATD. She has been featured in dozens of publications, including *The Wall Street Journal, Harvard Management Update, The Washington Post,* and *Fortune* magazine.

As a management and executive consultant, trainer, and designer, she has provided services to Outback Steak House Restaurant Group, FAA, Land O' Lakes, McDonald's, Lands' End, General Casualty Insurance, Chrysler, Johnson Wax, PricewaterhouseCoopers, American Family Insurance, Marathon Oil, Hershey Chocolate, Federal Reserve Bank, the U.S. Navy, NASA, Newport News Shipbuilding, Kohler Company, ATD, American Red Cross, Association of Independent Certified Public Accountants, the University of Wisconsin, The College of William and Mary, ODU, and hundreds of other public and private sector organizations to prepare them for the challenges of the new millennium.

She is the author and editor of over four dozen books and articles, including *ASTD's Ultimate Train the Trainer* (2009); *10 Steps to Successful Training* (ASTD, 2009); *The Consultant's Quick Start Guide* (2nd ed.) (2009); *ASTD Handbook for Workplace Learning Professionals* (2008); *Trainer's Warehouse Book of Games* (2008); *The Business of Consulting* (2nd ed.) (2007); *Thriving Through Change: A Leader's Practical Guide to Change Mastery* (2007); *Successful Team-Building Tools* (2nd ed.) (2007); *90 World-Class Activities by 90 World-Class Trainers* (2007) (named a Training Review Best Training Product of 2007); a nine-volume set of ASTD's *Certification Study Guides* (2006); *12 Habits of Successful Trainers* (ASTD Info-line, 2005); The ASTD Info-line *Dictionary of Basic Trainer Terms* (2005); *Training for Dummies* (2005); *Marketing Your Consulting Services* (2003); *The Consultant's Legal Guide* (2000); *Interpersonal Skills: Understanding Your Impact on Others* (1996); *Building High Performance* (1998); and *The Pfeiffer Annual: Consulting* and *The Pfeiffer Annual: Training* (1998–2010). Her books have been translated into Chinese, German, and Dutch.

Elaine has a bachelor's degree from the University of Wisconsin-Superior in business and education consulting and a master's degree in human resource development. She is active at the national level of ATD, is a life-time member, served on the 1990 National Conference Design Committee, was a member of the national ATD Board of Directors and was the society's secretary from 1991 to 1994, initiated and chaired Consultant's Day for seven years, and was the international conference design chair in 2000. In addition to her work with ATD, she has served on the Independent Consultants Association's (ICA) Advisory Committee and on the Instructional Systems Association (ISA) board of directors.

Elaine is the recipient of the 1992 National ASTD Torch Award, the 2004 ATD Volunteer-Staff Partnership Award, and the 2006 ATD Gordon M. Bliss Memorial Award. She was selected for the 1995 Wisconsin Women Entrepreneur's Mentor Award. In 2001 she received ISA's highest award, The ISA Spirit Award. Visit her website at www.ebbweb.com or contact her at ebbiech@aol.com.